STRATEGIES FOR
BETTER THINKING

STRATEGIES FOR BETTER THINKING

An Advanced Model for
Organizational Performance Consultants

Gerry H. Waller
Kathy A. Nielsen

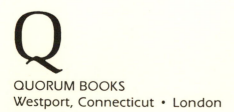

QUORUM BOOKS
Westport, Connecticut • London

Library of Congress Cataloging-in-Publication Data

Waller, Gerry H., 1951–
    Strategies for better thinking : an advanced model for
organizational performance consultants / Gerry H. Waller, Kathy A.
Nielsen.
      p.   cm.
    Includes bibliographical references and index.
    ISBN 1-56720-199-7 (alk. paper)
    1. Business consultants. 2. Performance standards. 3. Creative
thinking. 4. Group problem solving. I. Nielsen, Kathy A., 1949– .
II. Title.
HD69.C6W338   1999
658.4'036—dc21   98-30536

British Library Cataloguing in Publication Data is available.

Library of Congress Catalog Card Number: 98-30536
ISBN: 0-56720-199-7

First published in 1999

Quorum Books, 88 Post Road West, Westport, CT 06881
An imprint of Greenwood Publishing Group, Inc.
www.quorumbooks.com

Printed in the United States of America

The paper used in this book complies with the
Permanent Paper Standard issued by the National
Information Standards Organization (Z39.48–1984).

10 9 8 7 6 5 4 3 2 1

Copyright Acknowledgment

The authors and publisher gratefully acknowledge permission for use of the following
material:

Excerpts (submitted) from *What a Great Idea!*, by Charles "Chic" Thompson. Copyright
© 1992 by Charles "Chic" Thompson. Reprinted by permission of HarperCollins Publishers,
Inc., in the United States, its dependents, Canada, Philippine Islands, and the open market.
Reprinted by permission of the Sagalyn Agency in all other territories.

Contents

Acknowledgments

Our sincerest thanks go to all the people who contributed useful information and examples of their thinking strategies. Comments, thoughts, and ideas resulted from numerous discussions, client consultations, and training sessions where various aspects of thinking were presented. Hundreds of people shared in one way or another their experiences, needs, concerns, and frustrations, which helped us clarify and develop some sense of order to the "thinking" dilemma.

As each chapter of the book was drafted, additional questions, ideas, examples, and anecdotes were discovered from further discussions with friends, family, clients, and colleagues. Many of these were then formulated and added to particular chapters. The overwhelming task of sorting these wonderful comments and using them in a fashion that would add greater depth and breadth to the book's concepts was a tremendous challenge during completion of the final manuscript.

In particular, we would like to thank Paul and Brenda Buchik, John and Michelle Cassin, Helen Hazlett, Brad and Sarah Marsh, Thomas Quinn, Chet Staples, Albert Viehman, Bill and Bernadene Wood, and Rich Zappen for the time they took to offer ideas and suggestions at various times during the creation of this book. Whether it was helping to formulate concepts when the idea for the book was originally conceived, brainstorming theories and opinions, furnishing examples of their own thinking strategies, or simply providing encouragement, their support and cooperation is greatly appreciated.

Kathy Nielsen would especially like to thank Al Viehman, colleague and husband, whose practical thinking and managerial wisdom added insights in regards to the potential reader's experience and application of the model in the "real world"; also, Mary Wacker, a trusted colleague and deep thinker, whose consulting experience and willingness to discuss applications offered an objective viewpoint of various concepts.

Gerry Waller would like to extend his thanks and appreciation to Eric Valentine, publisher of Quorum Books for his belief in *Strategies for Better Thinking*, and his continuous support, encouragement, coaching, and professionalism throughout the creation of this book. Above all, he extends his thanks and gratitude to his wife Margaret and daughters Melissa, Colleen, and Courtney for their patience and love, which kept him focused on researching, developing, writing, and accomplishing this book and achieving his desired outcome.

Introduction

Just think. . . think about it. . . what were you thinking?. . . think again. . . a penny for your thoughts. . . think tank. . . group think. . . give me a moment to think. . . think it through. . . lost in thought. . . what do you think?. . . let me think about it. . . great minds think alike.

When we hear or use any one or more of these kinds of expressions, it tends to emphasize how powerful the thinking process is, and what an enormous role it plays in every single moment of every day of our lives. In fact, the ability to engage in high-level cognitive functions—thinking—is what sets human beings apart from the rest of the animal kingdom. Scientists have been studying the brain and its physiology and functions for centuries, and we know so much more about neurology and brain chemistry than ever before. Engineers and systems technicians have modeled computers after human thought processes. Psychologists have delved into the human mind to help their patients make connections between thoughts and feelings. Theologians and philosophers through the ages have persistently studied life's most complex questions and problems. In more recent years, there has been a plethora of books on creativity, imagination, memory improvement, the controlling of feelings, and even mind control.

Why then, does the thinking process remain such a mystery to us all? Why do we ponder, mull over, chew on, wonder about, and examine our thoughts, decisions, problems, and ideas? What does it mean to be a "deep thinker"? How does one get "found" when lost in thought? Why do groups "brainstorm" in business? What makes the difference between a "sound decision" and one less certain or more risky? If we know more, why are we not making better decisions all the time? With so much information about how to operate our own personal cognitive "software," how can we get the most from that software on a daily basis? Are there ways to improve our thinking that will make us more successful in whatever we do? These are just a few of the questions that are continuously presented when the subject of thinking comes up.

When we pick up the daily newspaper, browse through a magazine, read the current best-selling novel, listen to children describe what they learned in school, or attempt to master the current upgrade of some software package, we begin to realize the importance of thinking. We also become aware of the magnitude of thinking styles and strategies, and how many different ones can be useful to us. Expanding our thinking repertoire is not only deeply satisfying, it is critical to success and quality of life for ourselves and for our organizations. Consider what others have said about the importance of knowledge and thinking.

> The intellectual assets of a company are often worth three or four times the company's tangible book value.[1]
>
> NICHOLAS MOORE,
> Chairman and CEO of Coopers & Lybrand,
> *Chief Executive*, May 1997.

> Corporations are like monsters: heads enough, but no brains.
>
> BEN FRANKLIN

> No one is teaching workers how to think.[2]
>
> EARL HUNT,
> Professor of Psychology and Computer science,
> University of Washington—Seattle,
> *Will We Be Smart Enough? A Cognitive Analysis of the Coming Workforce.*

> There's a growing imbalance between the supply of smart people and the demands of the workplace, a workplace where problem-solving skills and the sort of fluid intelligence. . . will be desperately needed to meet the challenges at work and to figure out new ways of doing things.[3]
>
> DAVID STAMPS,
> Associate Editor,
> *Training*, April 1996.

Thinking more effectively makes us feel better about ourselves and our decisions and can help us manage changes within our personal and professional lives. Thinking more effectively can help us look at things from others' points of view and be more flexible in relationships. Thinking more effectively can save us time, money, stress, and energy and can help us gain respect, credibility, clients, and valuable insights. Thinking more effectively offers us challenges, opportunities, and benefits that can positively change our lives.

To engage in the thinking process involves a great deal of physiological functioning, much too complex for many of us to even fathom—nerve synapses firing at tremendous rates of speed, chemicals flowing from one part of the brain to another, storage and retrieval capabilities more intricate than any computer could ever be, and DNA lending its unique fingerprint to each of our thought processes. Had we chosen scientific research as our profession or avocation, we might have tapped into a greater knowledge and understanding of the thinking process long before now and perhaps would have taken it for granted. As a result, we might never have considered investigating thinking from a performance consulting perspective. We might never have challenged ourselves to pursue the existence of thinking strategies and processes and to write a book like *Strategies for Better Thinking*.

To some people, reading or writing a book about thinking is simply an esoteric exercise that attempts to segment and describe an incredibly complex process. However, we have learned over the years that it is possible to examine and document many complex processes, including those associated with communication, change, decision making, and many more. Why not thinking? The most consciously and unconsciously used human capability is that which we often give the least attention to and take for granted as "just there." We can all learn from those profound thinkers whose work we admire and seek to emulate. We can analyze, assess, and model the thinking strategies they used successfully, but, in the end, it is important to realize and appreciate the fact that we are not them, we are uniquely ourselves. We must learn to be a great thinker in our own way.

Over the years, we have consulted, coached, and trained individuals from many diverse organizations and situations. In the process, we discovered that most people give little thought or consideration to the actual process of thinking. Most people have rarely taken time to evaluate how thinking works, when it doesn't, or why one thought precedes another. Few people have taken time to understand why one person thinks he has clearly communicated a certain message, and another person in the same situation develops an entirely different meaning, or why some of us can reach a very different conclusion when thinking about some issue or problem. Rarely do people take time to consider what to do to align their thinking with others, how to identify and apply their thinking strategies in different contexts, or how to keep all their thinking from spiraling into one giant heap when there is so much "brain work" to be done. With so many people taking thinking for granted, or not taking the time to understand and develop their thinking, we felt compelled to do something that would help rectify the situation. We evaluated the characteristics of many great thinkers, studied various components of thinking, and formulated a model that could be used to identify and apply one's own thinking strategies. Our hope is that in the years to come, we encounter more and more people who not only know how thinking occurs but can quickly recall and apply the most appropriate thinking strategy for any situation.

Each of our thinking strategies is unique to us; yet patterns exist, overlap, and can become obvious to us and those around us when we make ourselves aware of their existence. We use those strategies that become natural to us and have, in most cases, gotten us through life with a measure of success. We take those strategies for granted, we count on our thought process to work for us as it has in the past, and we rarely clarify exactly how and why we employ the strategies we do. But consider the person who suffers even a mild stroke. Suddenly the manner in which that individual thinks and processes information, and then expresses those thoughts, can become a total mystery. Things once clear and easily remembered become vague or nonexistent images. Memories slip behind a veil and are not quickly projected onto the brain's visual screen, able to be reviewed and shared. The frustration of trying to formulate a single, simple thought becomes more difficult for the stroke victim than developing the theory of relativity was for Einstein.

Strategies for Better Thinking was written to teach people how to identify and apply unique yet natural, thinking strategies on their own. We don't use games and memorization techniques to make people more creative or better problem solvers (although these could be outcomes). We don't tell people how many different types of intelligence they should have (although some will discover new potential through the exercises on intelligence). We don't present numerous facts and figures about the brain (although an overview is provided that includes details relevant to thinking). We don't offer a single formula or technique that promises better thinking if it is applied in some specific way. We don't evaluate or judge the thinking strategies that we have experienced and those we know exist in every person. We do emphasize that each one of us has our own unique thinking strategies, and we offer ideas and examples for identifying and using them to our best advantage. We do emphasize that the approach described in *Strategies for Better Thinking* is the most advanced approach we know of for learning *how* to think and how to think more effectively.

Strategies for Better Thinking grew out of a vision and desire for helping people become more powerful and effective thinkers, so they could more easily improve their own performance and productivity and that of their organizations. Our memories go to discussions and comments overheard from frustrated executives and managers who wondered what their employees were "thinking" when they took a specific course of action or made a certain decision. Our recollections are of staff personnel, team members, and training participants who wanted to know what their managers and CEOs were "thinking" when they set priorities or took the company in a particular direction with seemingly little connection to the core business. We also recall our own experiences with clients, consultants, trainers, vendors and suppliers, and employees and staff whose thinking processes seemed so different from our own regarding some very basic issues.

To appreciate the thinking process that we each engage in; to identify its stages and boundaries; to call upon a specific stage in the process when working through a tough problem; to eliminate any portion of the process that is nonproductive in one situation and then use it in another—all are benefits of strategies for better thinking, and the exercises we have included throughout this book. We have used observations, questions, exercises, and activities, along with examples of how thinking strategies are identified and applied by others, to help develop an understanding and practical application of our strategies for better thinking model in personal and professional lives.

Strategies for Better Thinking provides a model that helps us

Discover the natural thinking strategies we use and those used by others.

Examine certain thinking strategies used by people who are considered great thinkers.

Find ways to expand our thinking beyond existing capabilities.

Examine what constitutes productive thinking for ourselves and others.

Explore creative methods for developing an awareness for our thinking strategies.

Recognize and understand the thinking strategies and patterns of other people.

Identify the thinking strategies that are most productive in different situations.

We apply the strategies for better thinking model to maximize our natural thinking strategies. Each of us has the ability to think clearly and powerfully, yet most of us have never been taught how to identify and use our natural thinking abilities. Equally important is the fact that most of us have not been encouraged to try new and different thinking strategies on for size and expand our repertoire in order to increase performance and achieve greater potential.

Strategies for Better Thinking enables us to identify and understand not only our own distinctive thinking strategies, but those of others whose strategies may differ. It also encourages us to adapt our capabilities to various contexts. *Strategies for Better Thinking* provides various techniques and exercises that uncover our natural capabilities, so we can think better, create easier solutions, generate ideas faster, and increase our total level of performance.

Strategies for Better Thinking is meant to provide ideas, questions, concepts, and applications that can help stimulate an understanding of our thinking strategies. Bringing thinking strategies into our conscious awareness helps us examine how they work, why they work, when they work, and how and why they don't work. As we move through the strategies for better thinking model, our levels of conscious and unconscious competence rise dramatically. We learn to use our strategies (and those of others) consciously so that they eventually become internalized and happen unconsciously, but with greater clarity, understanding, and productivity.

Any person with a desire to increase thinking for themselves and others can benefit from the contents of this book. Our vision is that *Strategies for Better Thinking* will impact and improve a large and diverse number of peoples' thinking. The more people who know about and share the strategies for better thinking model, the better. Providing our experiences, examples, and insights will hopefully provide others with the opportunity to learn, grow, improve performance, and enhance the quality of life. By sharing the strategies, techniques, and knowledge we have gained from our work with people inside and outside organizations, we hope to enhance our collective abilities, provide new and important insights to service client needs, and expand our repertoire of skills and resources.

Making our vision a reality meant getting *Strategies for Better Thinking* into the hands of people who already take thinking seriously, and who are interested in helping others improve those capabilities that achieve greater results. Performance consultants and others who take performance seriously fit that profile perfectly. Our many years of researching and studying thinking, designing examples and exercises, and formulating applications and uses for the model would be fruitless unless others had the opportunity to learn what we learned, use the knowledge to improve their lives, and become more accomplished thinkers. In our opinions, performance consultants provide the most logical and natural vehicle for helping others improve thinking.

As performance consultants, our "product" is a combination of our intellect, knowledge, experience, logic, process-orientation, problem-solving abilities, and creativity. Our clients rely on us to bring these products to them in order to examine their organizations and their people and to increase performance and productivity. If one book could help us leverage our unique knowledge and experience with clients in ways that make us more credible, more valuable, and more successful, wouldn't we take the time to read and work through the exercises and examples that are found within its pages? Of course, the answer for most people would be "yes." That's what we hope to accomplish with *Strategies for Better Thinking*—to provide a learning experience that performance consultants and others can use to achieve levels of performance never before thought possible. To accomplish this, we have attempted to go beyond the concepts of intelligence, creativity, problem solving, or how the brain works. Those types of books have already been written numerous times in the past and continue to be revised and updated today. We determined the need in our own work as performance consultants to take thinking to a greater level of understanding—one that truly develops an understanding, appreciation, and use for our unique thinking strategies and those of others.

In an economy driven by quality and service, remaining competitive consists of meeting the never ending needs and demands of customers in a fraction of the time provided by competition. It also means continuously upgrading technology, improving processes, and developing the skills and thinking of people. Therefore, our performance consulting efforts need to identify, develop, and continuously apply the primary "technology" that is available to us—our thinking strategies. Achieving a competitive edge and adding value to the products and services we provide requires thinking that goes beyond creativity and memorization techniques, brain teasers, and intelligence tests— it requires *Strategies for Better Thinking.*

NOTES

1. Nilly Ostro, "The Corporate Brain" *Chief Executive* May 1997, 58.
2. David Stamps, "Are We Smart Enough For Our Jobs?" *Training* April 1996, 47.
3. Ibid.

Chapter One

Strategies for Better Thinking

One of the most rewarding things we do as performance consultants is to help people improve their thinking. Over the years, we have taught people how to think to solve problems, memorize and retain information, influence others, and be more creative. All of us in the field of performance consulting must have been successful in our efforts over the years, because the awareness and acceptance for continuously improving one's thinking has become an important objective for more and more people. Also, the level at which people want to improve their thinking has continuously increased, so today we are finding that many individuals want to learn more than just someone else's strategies for solving problems, memorizing, or being more creative. Their level of sophistication for better thinking has evolved to a point where they want to learn how to identify and clarify their own strategies for thinking, and then apply those strategies in various contexts.

We know people have the capacity to think better. We also know that many people have never been taught to recognize and interpret their strategies for thinking. The ability to understand, use, and apply thinking effectively is considered by many to be a special gift that is available only to a few "exceptional" thinkers.

Various things come to mind when we discuss exceptional thinking. To some, exceptional thinking is represented by a person like Albert Einstein, Thomas Edison, Leonardo da Vinci, or by a song writer, actor, or sports figure. For others, exceptional thinking is defined by certain characteristics—like the ability to solve a complex mathematical equation, the talent to create an opera or movie score, or the skill to excel at some sport. Whether it is a person or characteristic, many people consider exceptional thinking to be something reserved for only a few highly talented people. It's not! Every person capable of thinking has the capacity for exceptional thinking.

Over the years, we have determined that exceptional thinking is simply the ability to recognize and appreciate our total mental capacity, so that we can apply the appropriate strategies for thinking in numerous contexts. When the people with whom we work accept this mind set, they begin to recognize that they already have what it takes to be exceptional thinkers, they just need direction for identifying and applying their strategies for thinking. When we maximize our natural thinking strategies and then put those strategies into practice, we exhibit characteristics that most people will consider exceptional.

Many of us consider an exceptional thinker as anyone who can do something that we do not consider ourselves capable of doing. Think about that. When we encounter someone who can do something that we don't think we can do, isn't our reaction something like, "Wow, I wish I could think like that!" When someone solves a complex problem, or creates a masterpiece, or exhibits highly efficient skills, we are very likely to consider that person to have a level of thinking that is far beyond our own capability. We all have the capacity for exceptional thinking—achieving it is simply a matter of identifying and applying thinking strategies that result in greater mental capacity.

To fully introduce strategies for better thinking, it is useful to establish a definition for thinking. Essentially, we define thinking as the process used to manipulate all of our memories, beliefs, values, experiences, and acquired knowledge to accomplish a specific outcome. It's a process that for most of us requires a set of actions accomplished in a particular order to get a desired result. Thinking is also a powerful skill that we can continuously improve, advance, and master. So, if we go through life without any realization of what our set of actions and specific order for thinking are, then we will significantly limit our capacity for exceptional thinking.

There are numerous opinions and ideas that exist about "thinking." However, most of what has been written and taught is limited to such things as how the brain works, how to memorize, and how to be more creative. Unfortunately, what is missing is specific information that teaches us how to think, how to identify and make the most of our own strategies for thinking, and how to apply our thinking strategies in ways that make us more effective. That's why *Strategies for Better Thinking* was written—to help people recognize their capacity for exceptional thinking and to help maximize their natural thinking strategies.

Thinking is a very subjective process, meaning that every person uses his or her own systematic series of actions directed to some desired outcome. Each of us has had various levels of successes and failures that have established our approaches to thinking. Such things as our experiences, educational backgrounds, and choices in life have developed, reinforced, and modified our specific thinking strategies. What works well for one person is very likely to be totally different from what works well for another. As a result, we have written

Strategies for Better Thinking as a system that can easily be used to identify, apply, and improve our particular thinking strategies. It is also a system that can help us identify what we consider to be the useful thinking strategies of others and apply them to our own situations. From a performance consulting standpoint, it is also a system that can be taught to others primarily for the purpose of helping them identify and apply their thinking strategies in ways that achieve significant advances in performance.

Because thinking is subjective and highly personal, the capability to establish scientific results that can be generalized from traditional research is fairly difficult. Therefore, we are continually gathering data and techniques that we encounter in discussions with various individuals and groups to develop an awareness and classification of various thinking strategies that exist. We encourage you to do your own research about how and when you think most effectively, and how others' thinking strategies can be adapted to enhance what you and your clients naturally do now.

Everyone has a brain. Everyone thinks. Except for those with brain damage or disease, everyone has the inherent ability to think effectively. *Strategies for Better Thinking* provides a method for identifying and understanding how we think—to maximize our natural thinking strategies in more powerful ways. Once we become aware of our thinking strategies, our ability to recall them quickly and use them in various situations is greatly enhanced. The result is a significantly higher level of performance and productivity.

Strategies for Better Thinking is a synthesis of techniques, activities, and exercises that help us evaluate our own strategies so we can continuously determine the strategies we are using and the actions we take when we think. For example, what exactly do we see, hear, feel, and do? When does our strategy work at its highest efficiency and when does it fail us? Because thinking is as automatic as breathing or walking and because it happens very quickly, we need an opportunity to slow down the process and fully examine it to understand exactly what is occurring. *Strategies for Better Thinking* enables us to find out how to identify the elements of our thinking strategies and those of others. It helps us clarify and develop an understanding of when it happens, how it happens, and exactly what happens.

Using the strategies for better thinking model, we assess and practice our thinking strategies from different perspectives and in different contexts. It also gives us a framework for trying out and practicing the thinking strategies of others. The model is not intended to confine us or force us into a particular method or approach. Rather, it is a way to expand our thinking options while trying out numerous strategies other than our own.

Strategies for Better Thinking can help us identify and understand our distinctive thinking styles, recognize our approaches to thinking, and learn to adapt our thinking capabilities in various contexts. We have included specific techniques and application exercises that can uncover approaches to thinking so we can think more clearly, create solutions more easily, generate ideas faster, and increase the total performance capabilities of ourselves and others.

BENEFITS OF STRATEGIES FOR BETTER THINKING

This book is an exploration in understanding, identifying, and developing thinking strategies for us and others. It can help us unlock our potential for thinking better. It can help us maximize our natural thinking strategies to achieve peak performance. It can even enhance our capacity for exceptional thinking and increase the value of our intellectual capital.

The benefits derived from our exploration will depend upon a number of variables, including the expectations we establish for ourselves; our level of involvement in the activities and exercises; our commitment to continuous practice and application; the effort we put into making positive changes for ourselves; and how much fun we decide to have. All of us will know the benefits of *Strategies for Better Thinking* have been realized when we hear people describe their experiences in ways such as "My thinking process and strategies have become distinct and clear to me. I am now able to direct my thinking in new and more satisfying directions," or "Because of *Strategies for Better Thinking*, my level of creativity and innovation is dramatically higher," or "After applying the model of *Strategies for Better Thinking* to my work, I now make faster and better decisions," or "*Strategies for Better Thinking* has helped me change the negative beliefs and perceptions I had about my capabilities for great thinking."

Peter Drucker has said, "The knowledge society will inevitably become *far more competitive* than any society we have yet known—for the simple reason that with knowledge being universally accessible, there is no excuse for nonperformance."[1] Consider too, that a large percentage of Fortune 1000 companies have been establishing the position of "Knowledge Officer" within their organizations and are implementing programs for capitalizing on their people's knowledge and intelligence. From a performance consulting standpoint, the benefits of strategies for better thinking are tremendous, especially with the concepts of knowledge and intelligence becoming so critical to an organization's continuous growth and survival. It is imperative that we, as performance consultants, not only stay ahead of this trend but also help develop and advance the trend.

Achieving greater levels of performance from knowledge and intelligence will not occur simply from the establishment of knowledge officers in organizations, or from the implementation of particular creativity techniques or gimmicks. Rather, it requires teaching every individual how to learn, apply, and share his or her unique thinking strategies so that knowledge and intelligence are turned into opportunities for greater performance. We cannot think creatively if we don't know how to think.

There are hundreds, even thousands, of thinking strategies that exist within every organization. Every person at every organizational level and function carries around untapped intellect and thinking strategies. When people are taught how to identify, access, and apply their unique thinking strategies, organizational intellect and greater performance quickly become realities. For example, opportunities are recognized faster; a greater number of ideas are generated throughout organizations; newer and more innovative products are designed and introduced faster; and processes are improved and implemented more rapidly.

If there is still some hint of doubt about the positive effect that thinking has on performance, consider the following questions:

Will organizational performance increase———

———when a greater number of ideas are generated?

———when people realize how to identify and use their unique thinking strategies?

———when people apply productive thinking strategies versus unproductive ones?

———if opportunities are recognized at a faster rate?

———by recognizing and appreciating the differences among various people's thinking strategies?

———when the fear of coming up with new ideas and implementing them is reduced?

———if a greater amount of knowledge is developed, promoted and applied among organizational members?

———by increasing the ability to access and use information more intelligently?

Our experiences with strategies for better thinking have provided us with a resounding 'yes' to each of these questions, and we continue to discover more with every performance consulting assignment. Developing exceptional thinking and helping others enhance their natural thinking strategies and abilities is undoubtedly the most significant contribution to greater performance now and in the future.

TUNE-UP FOR STRATEGIES FOR BETTER THINKING

Every one of us has the ability to think clearly and powerfully. What is interesting about the way we think is the fact that we all do it differently. There is no one approach for thinking—there are various approaches. And each one of us uses one or more approaches for which we have become comfortable and accustomed. Unfortunately, very few of us have ever clarified the elements and characteristics of our thinking strategy. When do we encounter our most productive and exceptional thinking? How does our exceptional thinking develop and evolve? What exactly happens before, during, and after an exceptional thinking experience? These are some of the key questions used to develop a conscious awareness of our thinking strategies.

One element of a thinking strategy might be separating oneself from an issue or problem, so the act of separation actually assists in the creation of ideas. For example, after taking some time to try and solve a problem, a person may become stuck in generating ideas for a solution. Perhaps at the point of being stuck the person gets frustrated and decides to do something else. He or she decides to forget the problem and go play golf, read a book, watch television, or go to sleep. The act of "forgetting" about the problem actually helps the conscious mind relax, and allows the unconscious mind to provide the missing information. So, while doing something other than concentrating on the generation of ideas to solve the problem, the person gets the "Eureka!" effect that results in a powerful solution. That's the "when" of a thinking strategy. Most people can tell us without much hesitation the "when" part of their strategy. The parts that require more investigation and introspection are the "how" and "what" of their thinking. So it's essential for us to slowly and patiently elicit the details pertaining to each person's thinking using the strategies for better thinking model that can be learned quickly and adapted to various situations in our lives. The stages of the Strategies for Better Thinking model help us determine which elements combine to create the easiest, fastest and best ways of thinking. Also, because each of our approaches to thinking is so different, we can learn to identify and practice many other thinking strategies that might also work well for us in various situations.

We have found the strategies for better thinking model to be useful for developing natural abilities and strategies for thinking within ourselves and our clients. The model includes four stages: clarification, generation, prioritization, and activation. Before jumping right into the concepts and model of strategies for better thinking, though, we have found it useful for our clients to clarify the expectations and perceived benefits they have for improving their thinking. We use a series of questions and activities that act as a preparatory step for exploring and tuning up people's attitudes about thinking, while also developing some useful insights for themselves.

The "tune-up" is a great way to ease people into the process while helping them flex their mental muscles about thinking and thinking strategies. Since there are no right or wrong answers to the activities and questions, people begin to build a greater motivation for thinking, while also developing a preliminary understanding of their thinking process. Keep in mind, though, that these questions are ones that people have rarely, if ever, taken time to answer. The questions, exercises, and activities that follow are powerful and stimulating from the standpoint that people have to apply a great deal of thinking in order to develop their responses. Reactions vary depending upon the self-image that each person has about his or her thinking and the level of conditioning they have received from traditional educational practices. For example, some people feel compelled to respond as quickly as possible to questions and to identify one particular answer that they think will likely be considered correct—even when the correct answer is something that exists within each person.

Everyone who completes the "tune-up" questions, exercises, and activities will need time, support, and encouragement to develop thoughts and responses that have been held deep within their unconscious minds. Some will need more time, support, and encouragement than others. In any case, the "tune-up" should not be expected to be completed within a matter of a few minutes. It can take hours and sometimes days to accomplish meaningful results from the "tune- up." Try out the questions and activities for yourself to find out the insights that are obtained from your results.

We begin with several questions like the ones listed below to establish clients' expectations and help them develop an awareness about the ways they do and do not think. These help formulate a vision or desired outcome for better thinking, which is something very few people have ever done.

1. How is the idea of thinking better and enhancing your thinking strategies important to you?
2. What experiences have you had to make you want to think better *now?*
3. What areas of your life can be improved by better thinking?
4. What benefits can *you* achieve from better thinking?
5. What barriers might prevent you from fully exploring your thinking strategies, and how will you overcome those barriers?

Several examples of responses to these questions are provided:

1. How is the idea of thinking better and enhancing your thinking strategies important to you?

   "In a world that requires doing faster and more, thinking could easily become a lost art."

   "Better problem resolution [in a] shorter time."

   "It would help me become more spontaneous with ideas and decisions."

   "Creative thinking is a tool that can help me be more successful."

   "Learning to think better can open up new possibilities for me."

2. What experiences have you had to make you want to think better *now?*

   "A faster pace leads me to act too quickley rather than thinking and then acting."

   "Lack of interaction with others has caused me to not be as sharp as far as developing the thought process, almost what I would view as a lack of confidence of thoughts and ideas or almost a lazy thinker."

   "I have recently relocated to a new city and want to explore the market. I want to develop a new client list and want to do a needs analysis to see what training concepts might be saleable."

   "I want to find new ways to keep a long term relationship fresh and interesting."

3. What areas of your life can be improved by better thinking?

   "Enhanced communication by understanding how I and others think."

   "Increased personal productivity and financial status."

   "Better decision making."

"To build a strategic business plan for my business."

"To help me hone and prioritize my top ten life–relationship goals."

4. What benefits can *you* achieve from better thinking?

"A greater understanding and use of different ways of thinking."

"Higher productivity as a result of better and faster problem solving."

"More confidence in reacting to thoughts and ideas."

"Staying focused, because when I am excited about a subject I tend to generate ideas so quickly at various levels that I sometimes lose track of the central idea."

"Better business planning and goal prioritization. In the long term, I would like a template to use on an ongoing basis to help me think more creatively."

5. What barriers might prevent you from fully exploring your thinking strategies, and how will you overcome those barriers?

"Lack of time and lack of proper prioritization of urgent issues. I need to apply a better way to think about time and priorities."

"Fear of failure, fear of sales execution . . . are all things that may cripple my chances for success. To overcome these I need to do two things: first, convince myself that new business and a better relationship are the two top priorities in my life, and second, I need to explore what will happen if I don't work on these two things. For example, if I always do what I've always done, I will always get what I have always gotten."

After establishing expectations and awareness for thinking, it is useful for people to clarify and understand the characteristics of their thinking. We use three activities to accomplish this portion of the "tune-up." Activity 1 helps clarify past experiences with thinking. Activity 2 develops personal insights about thinking through problems. Activity 3 helps clarify the processes used when thinking.

We encourage our clients to stretch themselves and go beyond simply providing answers. There is much more to the activities than simply coming up with quick responses. Rather, it is useful to fully clarify previous experiences encountered with thinking, as well as the sequence of thinking in various contexts. Also, these activities can be more than paper and pencil exercises, by using other recording methods such as drawing or dictation to develop responses. Finally, we have found that some of the most dramatic insights result from accomplishing the activities in several steps. First, we encourage clients to respond to the statements and questions with the first thoughts that come to mind. Second, clients need to take time to "test" initial responses in actual situations and record the ways in which thinking occurred. Third, we want clients to revisit the initial responses and include the additional information that was discovered about thinking in actual situations.

Following each statement or question within the activities are examples of quick, initial responses from several clients. Keep in mind that the initial responses will have very limited detail from which thinking processes and strategies can be ascertained. This is acceptable because it is from the initial responses that we begin to gather and build more precise and meaningful information by probing further about actual thinking experiences. For example, a client may initially respond by saying that he or she did not remember seeing anything in his or her mind during a frustrating thinking experience. This might be true for some clients. However, for others it is discovered after further probing that there were certain images that appeared in their minds during particular thinking experiences.

Activity 1: Experiences with Thinking

We ask clients to record their thoughts for each of the following items. The word *thinking* is being used in its broadest sense, so we encourage our clients to give themselves latitude when answering. And we remind them that this is not a test!

1. *Describe a time when you were disappointed or frustrated with some aspect of your thinking. What exactly happened? What do you remember seeing in your mind? What do you remember hearing in your mind? What do you remember feeling?*

Here are several examples of responses to this item.

"I was trying to understand a forecasting system. I wanted to 'shut down' instead of thinking it through. I felt overloaded by the situation."

"Right now! I seem to be unable to quickly 'pull up' a time from my past when something disappointing or frustrating happened. I'm feeling helpless and frustrated."

"Over the years, I have made some poor decisions where I feel the process was jaded by emotion or a sense of urgency. I sold my business several years ago. When I finally decided on a buyer, I did not feel confident with the decision. As the due-diligence stages proceeded, I got several small indications that the buyer was wrong for the deal. I neglected to go with my instincts and continued through the process feeling my reservations were based on emotional ties to the business. I also felt more pressured and confused as the sales process continued. As it turns out, it was the wrong deal to make and my instincts were soon substantiated after the sale."

"I was at a client's office and we were brainstorming ways of presenting training material to a group of electrical engineers. I started shooting out ideas and my client looked at me as if I had two heads. While I am sure she was trying to be polite, I could read the disappointment in her face. I was devastated. I thought for sure she was losing faith in me fast and questioning her decision to hire me. I remember hearing her speak to me and her tone was tolerant but cautious. I started feeling trapped and, what's worse, 'brain dead.' I felt like I would never have another original thought again."

2. *Describe a time when you were proud and satisfied with your thinking. What exactly happened? What do you remember seeing? What do you remember hearing? What do you remember feeling?*

Several examples of responses to this item include the following:

"I had been managing a group of people who worked with a kind of manual system for order entry, and for years we worked around an ongoing problem that occurred intermittently and was supposedly unresolvable. While working after-hours one night, I was speaking with someone on the telephone about a totally different issue and a solution to the ongoing problem came to me without any effort. I don't recall hearing or seeing anything, I just felt very satisfied with myself."

"I got a group of customer decision makers to focus on the 'big picture' of what my company could do for them, rather than having them emphasize a variety of details that confused the discussion. I only remember seeing the people within the conference room and then recall saying to myself, 'This is going nowhere, I have to get them onto more meaningful issues.' I remember feeling a combination of delight, glee, and pride when the discussion got on track and I was able to get desired results."

"On numerous occasions, I have had people describe problem situations occurring within their companies. It seems this gets my creative juices flowing. The thought process triggered questions to analyze the situations while developing creative solutions to the problems. By receiving instant recognition of the ideas, I felt excited and confident. It also seemed to sharpen my thought process and create a craving for additional ideas, which also carried over to anything else I was involved in after the initial conversation, whether it was another conversation, my child's homework, or reading. It seems that once I am excited about an idea my mind tends to want to feed the idea with additional information and creates ways to entice the brain to think how to acquire and apply more information at various levels to that initial idea."

"I was heading up a training group that was going to present to a group of marketing managers at their national meeting. The client chose a western theme for the meeting and required my group to do a dress rehearsal on stage with sound, lights, and props. It appeared after about fifteen minutes of floundering that no one knew where to start on the process. I suddenly realized that we needed a producer to get the rehearsal rolling, and we needed a director to focus the people involved in the production. Calling on my past theater experience, I stepped in, assessed the situation, and gently but firmly took charge. I saw people happily give me reign, and I heard sighs of relief and gratitude for the direction. I felt good that I could contribute and felt proud that I could call on past experience to combine past success with present success."

3. *Based upon the negative and positive experiences you described, how would you define thinking?*

The following are examples of responses to this question:

"I would define thinking as a thoughtful, purposeful, guided process to explore alternatives or solutions. It is not necessarily a quiet experience; however, it helps me a lot to have no interruptions or time pressures."

"An emotional experience."

"Not too involved with the external world (senses) but my own evaluation of the situation elicited emotions."

"A process involving creative emotion guided by instinct."

"I would define thinking as a way of developing a plan. I would think of it as a way of prioritizing thoughts and using them in the most advantageous and efficient manner. I would describe it as giving birth to ideas."

4a. Consider your negative and positive thinking experiences as processes for thinking, that is, the systematic series of actions that resulted in the negative and positive experiences. To clarify your process, think back on the experiences you described in the previous questions. Then, ask yourself questions such as What do I see in my mind before, during and after my positive and negative thinking experiences? What do I hear? What do I do? How do I behave? Or, stretch yourself to develop and answer other questions that come to mind. Any questions that can help you clarify your thinking process will be useful.

Several examples of responses to this item include the following:

"I recall seeing a flurry of different scenes, and I changed where I looked and my posture. I had a hyper behavior."

"A positive experience seems to instill a sense of accomplishment, confidence, and awakens creativity. I find the ability to visualize a successful outcome. Generally, my overall personality is much more positive as a result. The results of negative experiences have caused me to lose confidence and question my thinking process. As a result, it has made my risk tolerance low and has caused me to over think and overanalyze opportunities. The negative experiences tend to reappear as part of the thought process, a reminder, especially as it applies to my career. These reminders can also alter my mood into a negative state."

4b. Now list or describe the primary characteristics of your thinking process during a negative experience. That is, what are the distinguishing traits or qualities of your thinking process that causes you to classify it as negative? For example, the characteristics of one particular client's thinking process during a negative experience was negative self-talk that created black and white images in her mind and gave her a slight feeling of nausea that caused her hesitation about moving ahead with the idea—the result was an experience that she defined as "negative."

Several examples of responses to this item include the following:

"Irritation, fidgeting, energy with no outlet."

"Emotional response (frustration, impatience), perseverance toward understanding, determined to force myself through the details."

"Frustration seems to be the primary characteristic of my thinking process during a negative experience. It seems that I am thinking in circles and cannot break out."

"Question, evaluate, review previous similar situations; evaluate level of risk; visualize negative aspects or outcome of decisions; anxiety; decide or present with reservations."

"My ability to think gets strained. My ideas stop coming, or I have a hard time being original. Rather than focus on the idea, I focus on the perceived negative results of the idea—'That's not good enough'; 'No one will like it'; or 'That's a stupid idea!'"

4c. *Now, list or describe the primary characteristics of your thinking process during a positive experience. That is, what are the distinguishing traits or qualities of your thinking process that causes you to classify it as positive? The characteristics of a positive thinking experience for the client described above were almost the complete opposite, with positive self-talk resulting in colorful moving pictures that gave her a feeling like an adrenalin rush in her chest that caused her to be motivated to move ahead with the idea. These characteristics resulted in her definition of a 'positive' thinking experience.*

The following are several examples of responses to this item:

"Focused, peaceful, wide awake, energized."

"Emotional response (pride, an 'ah-ha!' experience), turning my thinking outward to others for acceptance."

"During a positive thinking experience, the thinking process feels like it is rolling along smoothly and inspired."

"Question, evaluate, or generate–visualize ideas; visualize positive outcomes or results from decisions; stimulation of excitement; decide or present with enthusiasm."

"My head feels clear except for the pathway in which ideas flow. The flow feels prioritized and it is as if I just feel 'right' in what I am saying and doing. It's a natural feeling state of being; one in which I feel comfortable, energized, and excited. Sometimes people even have to slow me down so that they can grasp the concepts."

5. *What exactly do you say and do when you help someone else "think through" a problem?*

Here are several examples of responses to this item:

"Talk, think out loud, and ask questions to understand their perspective."

"Ask pointed questions and give suggestions."

"To think through a problem with someone, I try to get them to walk it through one step at a time."

"Get excited for the opportunity to contribute a positive result."

"Ask them to do one of two things. I either ask them to take me through the problem from beginning to end (all the while, jotting down notes of where possible 'root causes' exist), or I ask them to tell me the solutions they have already thought of and together with the person, we examine the pros and cons of each solution."

6. *What causes you to come up with a good idea?*

The following are several examples of responses to this question:

"Focusing on a desired outcome or goal."

"Talking the issue through with someone, or letting it sit for some time."

"When I come up with a good idea, it's because I have become familiar with the issue at hand and have 'chewed it over' with someone. It also seems that a change in surroundings helps."

"Getting excited about applying my creativity."

"Caring about what's going on, and having a stake in the outcome. It is also because I don't let nonimportant 'stuff' cloud my thinking. I clear my mind and focus on the problem and the need to have a positive outcome."

7. *If you were to create the ideal thinking process for yourself, what would it be? What steps would it include? Where would your best thinking take place? What would the environment be like? Don't limit yourself on this one. That is, if you have difficulty writing it out, then describe it in some other way. For example, Dictate it! Draw it! Paint it! Build it! Discover what's there! What do you see and hear? What feelings are evoked by your description? Where is it? When do you go there? Have fun!*

The following are several examples of responses to this item:

"My ideal thinking process would be: (a) picture the desired outcome, (b) plan the steps to take, (c) have a computer or paper in front of me for recording thoughts and images, (d) create a picture in my mind (I'm very visual) of the results, (e) be contented, peaceful, proud, and committed."

"I would be in a group of highly motivated people, using a 'brainstorming' format with someone else taking notes."

"It would involve creating a state of mind where I don't feel pressured by the decision or its outcome; where creativity, excitement, and analysis drive the result. I would like to be in an emotional state, feeling comfort and not anxiety with the decision. I feel my best thinking would take place somewhere warm, overlooking the ocean, with no distractions other than nature. It would be peaceful, relaxing to my mind, and freeing my body and mind of all tension."

"I would like to be able to set time aside to just 'think.' I would like a 'fun' room with toys and music and videos and any other stimulation needed to get me into a variety of frames of mind. I would like an idea board to post 'fleeting thoughts' (bits and pieces of ideas to be saved for later). If I could set this up, I would love to make idea generation part of my career. I would love to create and be part of a think tank."

Activity 2: Thinking through Problems and Ideas

There are two parts to this activity. First, we ask clients to identify a problem situation for which they need to develop a solution. It can be a work-related issue, personal issue, anything—as long as it has personal importance to each of them. Second, we have clients identify an idea that they have wanted to develop but have been unable to for any number of reasons—such as, they don't think it's a good one, they don't have all the details developed, or they think it's not worth developing.

Part 1: A Problem Situation.   Here, clients consider a problem situation and take time to fully think about it—first, as though it is entirely their problem and then second, as though it is someone else's problem. We emphasize that they should think about and describe how it *really is* a problem (for example, the negative things that result from the problem). Then, think about how it *really isn't* a problem (for example, the positive things that can come from it).

Clients are then given some time to list any solution ideas that immediately come to mind. At that point, we instruct clients to restate their problem to themselves and record additional ideas over a period of two days. On the third day, the clients are told to record any ideas and solutions that they consider having the greatest possibility for eliminating the problem.

After establishing ideas and solutions, we ask clients to think about and record their responses to the following questions: When and where did you develop the best ideas and solutions? How did you develop ideas and solutions? What were the differences between your thinking processes when you considered the problem entirely yours and then considered it someone else's? They also need to consider any other details of their experiences that should be recorded. For example, one particular client discovered that his desire to help others solve their problems was much stronger than his desire to solve his own problems. That discovery enabled him to adjust his thinking process so that when he encountered a problem of his own, he would think of it as someone else's. The result was an enhancement of his thinking process in that particular context. Excerpts from examples of responses include the following:

"I seem to develop my best ideas and solutions during midafternoon while sitting at the computer. Typing out ideas on the computer screen keeps my mind working and focused on the particular issue."

"I come up with some great ideas while doing yard work. That is a form of relaxation for me, and as I do it, I have a tendency to just let my mind flow. As a result, I start making connections between numerous different things and after a while these connections start to bring about ideas and solutions for issues that I have at work and in my life."

"It is easier for me to solve someone else's problem. I can look at it totally objectively and the answers are clear as to what I would do."

"When coaching someone else through a problem, emotions don't intercede and solutions are more clear. It is also easier to 'talk' it through versus just thinking it through myself. Coaching is somewhat easier because it provides a good sounding board."

"When a problem belongs to someone else, it is easy for me to be separated from it. Just because of this separation, the creative ideas can flow more easily for me. When the problem is mine, my first inclination is to have a 'knee jerk' solution (if any), and it is easier for me to become stuck in a rut. When I can break free of the ownership of the problem, then ideas flow. If I can't break free, then discussion with another person is very important to me for generation of ideas."

"The main difference between the two processes is that I felt freer to give opinions when I was solving for someone else. I also felt more readily open to express my feelings and be honest. As a result of being more honest when the problem was someone else's, I learned that maybe it's a strategy I should use when weighing possibilities."

Part 2: Developing Ideas.   In this part, clients are asked to consider an idea that they have conceived but have not developed or implemented. While the idea itself is important, the actual thinking process they used to come up with it has even greater significance. Also, the specific details and characteristics of their thinking that keeps them from developing the idea are also worth understanding. These are the things we encourage our clients to focus on in this part of the exercise.

We begin this part by asking them to think about and describe how and when they came up with the idea. Then, we want them to think about and formulate their reasons for *not* developing and implementing the idea. After those details are developed, we want them to think about an idea that they came up with and also developed and implemented. Specifically, we want them to develop distinctions between the two situations, and then clarify exactly how their thinking process differed between the idea that was not implemented and the idea that was implemented.

After establishing the details about their thinking process for each idea, it's time for the clients to develop responses to the following questions: When and where did you come up with each of the ideas? How did you come up with each of the ideas? What were the differences between your thinking processes when you did and did not develop and implement the ideas? What do you consider the significant reasons for developing and implementing the one idea over the other? We then ask them to go back to each question to consider any other details about their experiences that should be recorded. There is always some valuable insight that is added when the clients go back to record any additional details.

Some excerpts from examples of responses are as follows:

"I develop and implement ideas if I can accomplish the end result without a lot of persuasion of others, and when there are no complications caused by things I cannot control. When ideas become part of a larger and more troublesome issue, the chances are slim that I will take them to the end."

"There was a 'deadline' for the idea I developed and implemented. The one that wasn't implemented was just an 'idea.' One idea was suggested by management—my thinking was toward a strategy to implement. The other was an incomplete thought of my own that required some visual charting for me to move forward."

"Those ideas I have abandoned are usually because I did not have the commitment to overcome the obstacles to follow through. More recently, my last undeveloped idea was from a spur of the moment emotional base that seemed like a great idea at the time; however, it turned out that other emotional costs would be higher than I am willing to pay for now. My developed ideas are those where I had the commitment to follow through and overcome the obstacles."

"At this point in my life, I probably feel a low risk tolerance. . . I feel I don't want to start a new venture unless it can be adequately capitalized. I feel a certain comfort level with our savings and investments and less likely to take the risks. In the past, when I had a much higher risk tolerance, I found it much easier to develop ideas. As these ideas came into fruition, my confidence and creativity levels increased. I felt a sense of accomplishment upon reaching the goal, and eager to create the next plan of attack in developing another idea."

"Both ideas concerned life plans. Both had appeal to me as a way of measuring lifelong success and contribution. The theater group was developed out of a shared need for a group of people to express themselves and be with others in the creative process. That was truly the appeal—that I was not alone in this endeavor and that I could count on other people to motivate me and support me in building my dream."

Activity 3: Clarifying the Thinking Process

The purpose of this activity is to help clients begin clarifying the characteristics of their thinking process (or processes). Based on the details they have established from the previous activities, we ask them to describe the significant parts of their thinking process and the unique characteristics of each part. For example, the different mental processing that occurs when thinking about a problem versus developing and implementing an idea. Exactly what were the mental processing characteristics that occurred in each context? Did pictures or other visual images develop? Were there internal sounds or self-talk? Were there particular feelings that developed? What exactly were the distinguishing traits and qualities of each characteristic?

Some excerpts of responses from this item are as follows:

"I seem to know more about myself in terms of a decision-making process than a thinking process, but maybe there is no difference. Within the process there are many characteristics, among them are emotions, past experiences, visualization, timing, enthusiasm, pain–pleasure, and environment. I think there are two completely different thought processes used when comparing problems versus ideas. I find myself to be more enthusiastic and in a more positive emotional state while trying to be creative, and in a more analytical mode while problem solving, examining and dissecting options, trying to visualize pitfalls, and anticipating results."

"When it is just me, I find it hard to be motivated and keep going. I don't like working alone on big dreams and find it much more appealing as well as satisfying to share dreams. I guess the conclusion I could draw would be that I need to develop a thinking strategy that will include others so that I can be sure of support and motivation when I need it."

SUMMARY

Thinking is the process we use to manipulate all of our memories, beliefs, values, experiences, and acquired knowledge to accomplish a specific outcome. We all have the ability to think clearly and powerfully, yet many of us have never been taught how to identify and use our natural thinking strategies. Each day, there are numerous strategies we use and have become accustomed to in various contexts, and like those people considered to be exceptional thinkers, we too have the ability to recognize and appreciate our total mental capacity in order to apply appropriate thinking strategies.

Using a series of questions and activities, we accomplish a preparatory step that explores and develops people's attitudes and insights about their thinking. As a result of the "tune-up" questions, exercises, and activities, clients begin to become aware of some of their thinking strategies, the environments that tend to promote better thinking, and the sensory responses that occur to stimulate better thinking. While there might be some similarity to responses (such as many clients finding it easier to solve someone else's problem than their own), every client's response will be unique. That uniqueness should be encouraged and appreciated because it contributes to more precise understanding for the meaning within each client's responses. We develop further understanding of the client's responses through a relaxed and nonthreatening style of questioning—a conversational style that is totally nonjudgmental and displays a genuine interest in how each client's thinking strategies are accomplished.

NOTE

1. Peter F. Drucker, *Managing in a Time of Great Change* (New York: Penguin Books, 1995), 236.

Chapter Two

The Brain, Learning, and Thinking

THE POWER OF THE BRAIN

The brain is truly a wonder of nature, and much of its functioning remains a mystery to neuroscientists and researchers. Its capabilities for feeling, perceiving, thinking, and reasoning are highly complex and intangible. So, while researchers continue to learn how the intangible aspects of the brain work, we think it is important to at least determine our own strategies for thinking and develop ways to stimulate our thinking for greater results. Developing an understanding of what is currently known about the functioning of the brain helps us maximize our thinking strategies.

The brain is the most sophisticated computer we could own, capable of storing and processing tremendous amounts of information instantaneously. It also keeps us safe and alive by accomplishing bodily functions that generally go unnoticed. Yet, most of us take our brain for granted. Many of us exercise our bodies, but rarely stimulate the three-pound muscle in our head. We use less than 10 percent of our brain's capacity, and we fail to take full advantage of our brain's thinking power and capabilities. Most of us continually upgrade our personal computers to meet the information and application demands of today's highly technical society, but do not try to upgrade and learn about the computer we carry in our head.

There are numerous books that fully describe the parts of the brain, explain how certain portions of the brain operate, and what current research has discovered about the brain, and we encourage our clients to read those books and expand their knowledge about the brain. Our emphasis in this chapter though is to focus on four specific areas of information: the parts of the brain, the functioning of the brain, current knowledge about how the brain processes information, and exercises that some of our clients have found to be useful for stimulating brain activity. The purpose is to develop a greater understanding for how the functioning of the brain can affect and impact thinking strategies and vice versa. This understanding is useful as we progress through the remaining chapters.

Parts of the Brain

The brain stem, the cerebellum, and the cerebrum are the three levels of the brain, and each performs particular functions. These levels, and the major parts within each level, are shown in Figure 2.1.

Brain Stem.   The first level is the brain stem, which is an extension of the spinal cord. Through the medulla oblongata, the brain stem regulates the body's life sustaining systems, including respiration, blood circulation, and reflex movements. Surrounding the brain stem is the limbic system, which is made up of the thalamus, hypothalamus, pituitary gland, pineal gland, amygdala, and hippocampus.

Each part of the limbic system has certain responsibilities. The thalamus receives signals from the senses and interprets them for us. The hypothalamus

Figure 2.1
Parts of the Brain

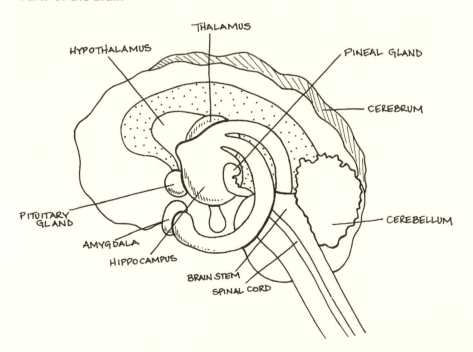

regulates our body's temperature and blood pressure, signals our level of hunger and thirst, and is also the repository of our emotions. The pituitary gland secretes hormones that affect growth and help our body produce energy from food. The pineal gland is believed to be responsible for the rate of growth and can also be activated by light and darkness. The amygdala, according to recent research, may moderate imagination and also trigger aggressive or docile emotions. The hippocampus helps us develop and store memories, and it also assists with simple recall.

Another part of the limbic system is called Reticular Activating System (RAS) which acts as a gatekeeper of information coming in from our senses. It filters sensory stimuli by allowing certain messages to take priority over others that pass through the brain. RAS is somehow capable of determining which messages are important at particular times and helps us concentrate and stay focused. For example, our RAS will help us notice a pedestrian stepping off the curb even though the stop light we are approaching is green.

Cerebellum.   The cerebellum is the second level of the brain, and protrudes from the brain stem. It has a distinctive arrangement of brain cells so that it can synthesize sensory information received from every part of the body. The cerebellum controls our body's motor and sensory movements. It gives our body balance and coordinates muscle tone and posture, as well as hand and eye movements.

Whether a person is kicking a soccer ball or typing on a computer, the cerebellum is the part that is making sure his or her muscles are working in the right ways to accomplish the activities.

Cerebrum.   The third level is the cerebrum, or sometimes called the "upper brain." It is the largest of all three levels of the brain, making up about 85 percent of the brain's total mass. The cerebrum is covered by an outer layer called the cerebral cortex, and the entire cerebrum is divided into two hemispheres—left and right—which are connected by the corpus callosum. Each hemisphere contains an intricate network of cells that receive, process and store information. The cerebrum is where thinking occurs—giving us the ability to reason and solve problems. The cerebrum is our warehouse for intellect, memory, language and the ability to understand symbols. It is also involved in motivation, emotion, levels of awareness, and the ability to experience sensation and movement.

Functioning of the Brain

The brain contains about one hundred billion brain cells at birth. The brain's basic unit is the nerve cell or neuron, and it contains between ten billion and fifty billion neurons. The remaining brain cells are supporting glial cells, which provide nutrients and maintain an optimal space between neurons. Each neuron is like a computer processor that sends and receives tens of thousands of messages per minute through electrical and chemical impulses. Every neuron has a unique, irregular shape, and consists of three parts: cell body (which contains the nucleus), long fibers called axons, and short fibers called dendrites. Figure 2.2 below illustrates the functioning of neurons.

When a neuron receives a message, it processes the message within the cell body. The message is then electrically transmitted along the length of the axon. As the message moves along the axon, it comes close to the dendrites of other neurons and is transmitted chemically across an immeasurably small gap called a synapse. The message is then converted back to an electrical impulse on the dendrite which transmits it to that neuron's cell body. The entire transmission occurs within milliseconds.

Figure 2.2
The Functioning of Neurons

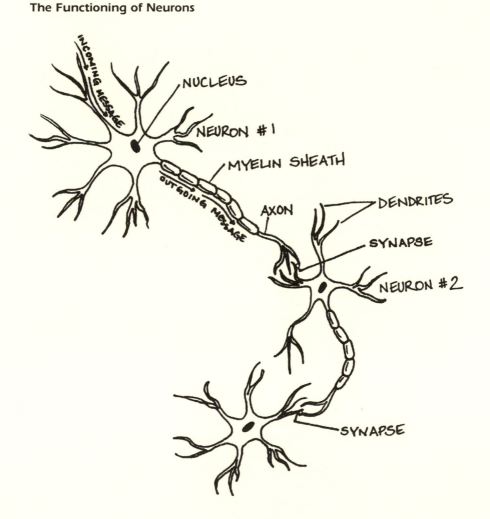

How the Brain Processes Information

It is the synapse that makes it possible for neurons to "communicate" with one another, and research has determined that synapses are very important to the processing of information, particularly in terms of learning and memory. One of the mysteries that neuroscientists have been investigating is exactly how synapses determine which messages get transmitted and in what order of priority. Another important area of research focuses on how continuous learning, stimulating environments, and creative thinking increase the strength and speed of activity that occurs at the synapse.

When we "exercise" our brains with a positive learning environment and stimulating activities, the glial cells split and duplicate. As a result, axons push through and create additional links between neurons. The result is a greater number of connections that can share messages. While the number of neurons in the brain will stay the same, the number of possible connections for sharing messages can be increased. The more we stimulate our brains, the faster the glial cells split and improve the functioning of synaptic structures.

The importance of brain stimulation is illustrated by a variety of studies, the most well known having been conducted by Mark Rosenzweig and Marian Diamond, both of the University of California, Berkeley. Dr. Rosenzweig's study involved comparing the impact of environments on brain development of two groups of rats. The first group was placed in an unadorned and ordinary cage, while the second group was exposed to a highly appealing and stimulating environment. The brains of the rats in the enriched environment grew larger and developed thicker concentrations of synapses.[1] Dr. Diamond's study involved the examination of a portion from the left hemisphere of Albert Einstein's brain, a portion that she believed to be responsible for math and language skills. She and her associates discovered that there were a greater amount of glial cells and synaptic connections within that portion of Einstein's brain.[2] There are, of course, other scientists who contend that it is highly unlikely to find intelligence or genius within Einstein's brain, or anyone else's for that matter, an attitude that we find very limiting in regards to future discoveries of brain functioning and thinking.

Exercising the Brain

While researchers continue to unlock and debate the secrets of how the human brain functions, we choose to follow the notion that our brains' processing capabilities can be significantly increased with stimulating environments, continuous learning, and creative thinking. Some scientists, such as Robert J. Sternberg at Yale University, consider as much as 50 percent of a person's intelligence to be determined by his or her past, present, and future environments.[3] Continuously challenging our minds and exposing them to stimulating environments will boost our brains' ability to receive and process information. Each of us has the power to increase the level of our intelligence throughout our entire life.

Our challenge is to determine the environmental characteristics that give us positive stimulation. Then, once determined, we need to regularly expose ourselves to those stimulating characteristics. For example, one of our clients was extremely proud of the awards and educational degrees and certificates he had received over the years. These were very strong sources of positive stimulation for him because they represented his achievements and reminded him of what he was fully capable of accomplishing. Still another client found his stimulating environment characterized by motivational quotes and stories. As a result, he would post numerous quotes on his wall and update them on a weekly basis, often creating his own quotations that further boosted his motivation and thinking.

A word of caution about recommending environmental stimulation, however, is in order. The characteristics of positive environmental stimulation will not be the same for every person, and it is extremely important for us to refrain from imposing our preferences on others. A stimulating environment for one person may be a stressful environment for another. While a particular individual may be stimulated by his awards and degrees, another person would find the same thing highly distracting.

There are numerous activities that each one of us accomplishes every day to stimulate our brain's processing capabilities. Unfortunately, the activities are usually limited to the ones we perform in our work or those that are used when we participate in some recreation or hobby. As a result, we tend to continuously stimulate the same portions of our brain, while other portions rarely get any "exercise." Therefore, it is necessary to develop an exercise program that regularly stimulates various portions of the brain that are not used as often as others. For example, if we are somehow actively involved with music, we would naturally exercise that area of thinking quite regularly. On the other hand, other areas of our thinking, such as conceptual or spatial, might be ones that would benefit from planned exercises. We use particular exercises that pertain to the following nine categories of thinking:

Auditory—This category involves sensitivity to internal and external sounds and the ability to recognize and distinguish the traits and characteristics of the sounds, as well as various aspects of language that include grammar and semantics.

Conceptual—This category is used to refer to the capacity for logical and abstract reasoning and the ability to solve mathematical problems.

Creative—This category involves originality of thought and imagination and the ability to create new forms, concepts, and interpretations that are useful in various applications.

Spatial—This category refers to the ability to accurately perceive the size and dimension of objects, as well as the space within and around objects, and also manipulate objects in the mind by changing their size, dimensions, or movement.

Visual—This category involves sensitivity to internal and external images and the ability to recognize and distinguish the traits and characteristics of the images.

Musical—This category refers to the ability to accurately produce or duplicate melody, rhythm, volume, and qualities of tone, as well as the ability to identify particular musical sounds and instruments.

Physical—This category involves the ability to perform and control movements of the body, and to carry and manipulate objects.

Interpersonal—This category refers to the ability to positively relate to others, including the ability to understand the behaviors, emotions, or actions of other people.

Independent—This category refers to the ability to confidently develop one's own thinking or actions without being influenced or controlled by some other person or group.

Descriptions of exercises for each one of the nine categories of thinking are described below. Try these for yourself and with your clients. Also, it may be useful to develop additional variations of exercises within each category.

Exercising for Auditory Thinking. Exercise 1: Sit in a comfortable position and have a pencil and paper ready to record results of the exercise. Take only five minutes each day for at least five days to listen for and list all the sounds (internal and external) you hear. As soon as you hear a sound, write it down. Stop when five minutes have passed and check your list to determine how many internal and external sounds you heard. Save your lists from each day to see if you were able to increase the number of sounds you heard from the first to the fifth day. For example, on the first day you may have only listed twelve sounds but by the fifth day your list of sounds had doubled.

Exercise 2: As you hear people talk, listen for various traits and qualities in their voices and compare those to your own voice traits and qualities. For example, is each person's voice louder or softer than your own; and is their pitch higher or lower than your own; is the tempo of their voice faster or slower than your own; is there a unique rhythm to the voices?

Exercising for Conceptual Thinking. Exercise 1: When presented with numbers that need to be added, subtracted, multiplied, or divided, work out the answer in your head first rather than using a calculator. Then, if you must, use the calculator to check your answer. Do this for several calculations each day.

Exercise 2: Design and make five different kinds of airplanes from the same size and type of paper. Then, test fly each paper airplane and identify one way that each design can be modified slightly to improve its performance.

Exercising for Creative Thinking. Exercise 1: Think about your job and determine five things that you could do to accomplish it easier, better, faster, and with more enjoyment.

Exercise 2: Find some popular board game, like checkers or backgammon, and create a different game using the same board and game pieces. You can also use a deck of cards and create a new card game.

Exercising for Spatial Thinking.   Exercise 1: Sit in a room (i.e., your kitchen, bedroom, or office), look around, and make a list of the various sizes and shapes of items in the room. Then, choose ten items and estimate the dimensions of each one. For example, what size is the rectangular toaster in your kitchen? What size is the round globe of the ceiling light? After estimating the dimensions, measure each one to check your accuracy.

Exercise 2: Think of how you could redesign the layout of your home or office. Sketch the layout on a piece of paper.

Exercising for Visual Thinking.   Exercise 1: Choose a place where you will be free from noise and distractions for at least five minutes. Sit in a comfortable position, close your eyes, and daydream. As you daydream, discover what kind of images and pictures come into your mind.

Exercise 2: Focus your sight on some object or picture for about thirty seconds. Then, close your eyes and describe the object or picture as it appears in your mind's eye.

Exercising for Musical Thinking.   Exercise 1: Briefly listen to a portion of a song. Then, turn off the song and hum or whistle the melody of the portion you had just heard. Do this with at least twelve different songs each time you do the exercise.

Exercise 2: As you watch a movie, listen for the background music that is played at various times. Determine how the music corresponds to the portion of the movie. For example, fast instrumental music being played with a segment that shows a lot of action.

Exercising for Physical Thinking.   Exercise 1: Slowly walk up and down a short set of stairs. As you do this, become aware of the portions of your body that are being used each time you go up the stairs and each time you go down the stairs.

Exercise 2: Stand in place. Begin by lifting your right hand and left knee into the air. Bring them down and repeat this with your left hand and right knee. Do ten repetitions of this step. Then, count off each repetition as you do the exercise at least twenty more times—that is, on the count of one lift your right hand and left knee and return, on the count of two lift your left hand and right knee and return, and so on. Then, replace the counting with the letters of the alphabet as you do five more repetitions. That is, on the letter 'A' lift your right hand and left knee and return, on the letter 'B' lift your left hand and right knee and return, and so on.

Exercising for Interpersonal Thinking.   Exercise 1: While in a group setting, such as a meeting, or party, listen to a conversation between two people and determine the meaning behind each person's statements. This will require you to listen attentively and then ask questions to establish each person's meaning.

Exercise 2: Over a period of four weeks, call sixteen people who know you but with whom you haven't spoken with in at least six months or more.

Exercising for Independent Thinking.   Exercise 1: Read the newspaper each day and select two stories that you consider controversial. Then, write your opinion either for or against one side of the story.

Exercise 2: Identify an idea or project that has been delayed or canceled, and establish a plan for how you could get it accomplished.

These are not meant to be exercises that are done once and then forgotten. Like any type of exercise program, we encourage our clients to maintain a commitment and regular schedule for completing the exercises. We emphasize that they need to be creative when scheduling and accomplishing these exercises. Also, creating new exercises or developing variations to the ones listed here is encouraged to further stimulate the brain and enhance the total exercise program.

LEARNING, THINKING, AND INTELLIGENCE

What do we think of when someone suggests learning something new? What pictures come into our mind? What do we hear, smell, and taste? What feelings and sensations occur in our bodies? Where in our bodies do the feelings and sensations occur? What are the similarities and differences between learning and thinking? What happens when we think? Are there strategies we use to make our thinking easier and more effective? These are all useful questions for stimulating our clients' understanding about their own opinions pertaining to learning, thinking, and intelligence, and the information provided in this section helps explore these questions and clarify what learning and thinking means to the people we work with.

Thinking about Learning and Thinking

Learning is a mental process that involves logic, intuition, perception, insight, and a connection of previous experiences with a current one. Learning is also a physical process that uses the brain in conjunction with all the senses. And, unless the brain has a physical impairment or we are allowing previous experiences to delete, distort, or generalize a current situation, we can *learn* anything! When it comes to learning and thinking, it is useful to remember that "we are the sum of what we make of our experiences," which is different from "we are the sum of our experiences."

We all have basic assumptions about the world, including how things work and how we fit in. These assumptions can give us stability, or they can become barriers when we no longer perceive the world without them and can't move beyond them. These assumptions begin to define us, restrain us, contain us, or move us to action.

We all have a collection of positive and negative perceptions about our personality, our intelligence and our ability to learn and think. These perceptions enhance or limit our achievement in very real ways. We are what we believe we are. The tragedy is that many (or all) of the negative perceptions may not be valid now—if, in fact, they ever were. So, we have found it very useful to ask people to consciously establish what they consider to be

their barriers to learning, and then determine details for how they have overcome those barriers in the past.

During our years of schooling, particularly the early ones, we learned to
read, write, add, and subtract, we learned who wrote the Constitution, and
what happens when we pour vinegar into baking soda. We also learned that
there was only one right answer—and that answer was protected by the teacher
until he or she thought we were ready to receive it.

We also learned to stand in line, wait our turn, speak only when spoken
to, and start when the teacher told us to begin. We learned that some kids
seemed smarter than others, and if we can't do math, well, there are other
things in life. We learned that learning is rote memorization and giving answers verbatim for a test. We learned not to question teachers. In fact, some
of us began to perceive that only certain people are qualified to teach and
some of the rest of us were given little opportunity to contribute.

Our years of schooling created different responses in all of us. For some,
the response may have been fear and anxiety about learning something new.
For others, the response may have been to show teachers and others that we
could learn using our own methods in spite of a single approach to instruc-
tional methodology. Still others may have been very pleased with the learning arrangement and comfortable with the way information was presented
and learning was tested.

The point here is that specific experiences have established our attitudes
and approaches to learning and thinking, as well as the perceptions we have
about our own capabilities for greater thinking—or even greater intelligence.
Therefore, we have found it very useful to help people clarify and understand
their experiences in order to enhance them as a basis for thinking.

To accomplish this, we use a series of statements that help our clients "revisit" the experiences they had encountered with learning and thinking in
school. Responses to the statements offer a variety of interesting descriptions
of learning and thinking experiences, some of which are positive, and some
that explain how people's current apprehensions about their real capabilities became established. What is important here is that the experiences,
whether they are mostly positive, mostly negative, or a combination of both,
have all contributed to each person's perceptions about his or her own "intelligence." When we accomplish this exercise with clients, we assist them in
their recall of learning and thinking experiences using the following steps
and ask them to record their experiences for each of the statements.

Learning Revisited.   First, recall some experience in grammar school—perhaps
kindergarten or first grade—that helped you determine what it meant to learn.
Now there may be several that come to mind, so just focus on one right now.
As you recall that one experience, remember what you saw, heard, and felt.
Take the time to *really* remember the experience, including your emotions
and reactions.

When you are ready, begin recording the details of the experience. Record the specific sights, sounds, and feelings from your learning experience. Then, record the negative as well as positive emotions and reactions that you felt because of that learning experience.

The positive and negative perceptions of learning that have been developed from our experiences have shaped our attitudes and confidence about thinking and intelligence. So now, describe the attitudes about learning that you presently have as a result of your early experience.

For some people, recalling their early experiences about learning will bring back certain negative emotions, while others recall mostly positive experiences, and still others recall a combination of positive and negative experiences. Feelings of fear and anxiety or joy and contentment are examples of the kinds of emotions that may have been encountered during our educational experiences. As a result, these experiences have established perceptions about our capability for learning and thinking. So, based on the perceptions of learning that were established from the previous exercise, we develop additional understanding by using the following questions.

1. In your opinion, what is learning?
2. How do you learn? That is, describe the process you use most often to learn something. For example, a person may use a four-step learning process that includes (a) receiving auditory instruction; (b) reading a text that provides information and examples about the topic being learned; (c) connecting the instruction and information received with personal experiences; and (d) teaching the topic to someone else. Still another person may primarily use only a two-step process where she reads about the topic to be learned and then applies the particular concepts in specific situations. What is the learning process that you tend to use most often? Take some time to think about and record your process.

Examples of responses to the previous questions include the following:

"Learning is the archival of information, facts, and experiences that develop thought patterns and decision-making techniques."

"I think that my learning is a three-step process. I receive information from numerous sources—text, visual, conversation, and experiences; I process the information; I visualize how the particular information can be applied to a situation, or should have been applied to a past experience."

"Learning is the ability to understand concepts of an idea, a situation, or a discipline, and be able to apply these concepts in a variety of situations."

"I learn the theory. This is done through study and application. I am a very visual person, so I need to then find ways to 'see' the concept or process as it stands alone, and then 'see' how it is applied in a given situation. I need to experience the idea in a context, and I need to feel the positive and negative aspects of the results of the concept in the context. I learn through seeing and feeling."

Thinking Revisited.   Albert Einstein once said, "My gift of fantasy has meant more to me than my talent for absorbing positive knowledge." In other words, he considered his ability to think and imagine a greater asset than the knowledge he had acquired. Learning is a dynamic activity with thinking being the highest order of learning. It is one of the most significant acts of human consciousness and unconsciousness.

Considering the distinctions between our perceptions of learning and those we have about thinking provides very interesting and revealing information. For example, we begin to discover that learning is primarily a process of taking in data and facts, while thinking is a process of internally organizing data and facts to reason and form opinions. We also begin to clarify some of the subtle differences between the ways in which we learn and think.

The questions in the previous exercises help formulate information about learning experiences. Our next step is to think about thinking by contemplating the following questions. Take some time to answer these for yourself.

1. In your opinion, what is thinking?
2. How do you think? Again, like you did for learning, describe your thinking process. For example, it's one thing to learn about the parts of the brain and how the brain functions. It's something else entirely to think about how you would use that information about the brain to improve yourself and the world around you. Therefore, a person's thinking process in the context of this example might be to (a) evaluate and imagine various ways of applying what he has learned; (b) take time to relax so that his thoughts and ideas about the subject have time to incubate; (c) come up with a useful idea for developing and improving his thinking; (d) apply, test, and modify the idea in various situations, and (e) select, practice, and apply the modified approach that achieves the greatest results. Describe a process you have used for thinking. Take some time to recall and record the thinking process you use most often.

Examples of responses to these questions include the following:

"Thinking is the processing function of the brain. It is the process by which we search the archives for ways to apply the information stored to a particular situation. In thinking, a level of creativity is used to visualize, imagine, or formulate the process."

"I consider myself an analytical thinker. Depending on my interests or anticipated result or need I tend to visualize the outcome, hopefully in a positive way. I feel I evoke a lot of emotion in my thought process and reviewing previous situations that appear similar. If it is an interest or topic that I am very excited about, I feel my creative emotions are heightened, the thinking process is much more fun, and I can almost think of nothing else. I do a lot of thinking in bed, and unless I get up and write down my ideas, I cannot fall back to sleep."

"In my opinion, thinking is the ability to have thoughts, recognize the thoughts, organize the thoughts, put them into a context, and then, if so choosing, act on the thoughts."

"I tend to think in two ways. The first way is to generate ideas and put them into scenarios and play them out to see and feel how the idea will work. The second way is to put the thoughts or ideas through a series of 'if–then' statements to try and visualize different outcomes. If I need to think about a particular issue, I find a quiet place, clear my head and prepare myself with a pen and pad of paper. I will start thinking about the ideas using my two ways described above and then as results start to appear to me, I write the options down on a piece of paper. Once I have them down, I will generate a pros and cons chart, choose the ideas that have the most chance of working, then organize them into a priority goal list. If I can be placed in a situation where someone else is in on the process, then the session turns to brainstorming and 'if–then' scenario application. A list of ideas is generated and then those of us involved decide what to work on and how."

Peak Thinking Experiences. Many have heard of Abraham Maslow and his "needs hierarchy." Besides his work in that area, Maslow also conducted research in what he calls "peak experiences."[4] A peak experience is that moment when our mind and body perform with total excellence and we *know* that whatever we attempt *will* be accomplished. Maslow noticed that many peak experiences tended to occur during times of intellectually demanding activities, such as learning, problem solving, and decision making. Therefore, we want to consider our peak experiences in relation to thinking and respond to the following questions. We encourage our clients to take time developing responses to this exercise. The responses will not only provide significant personal insight, they will also contribute to the application of concepts presented in later chapters.

1. What was a peak thinking experience for you? Describe where you were, what you saw, what you heard, and what you felt, smelled, or tasted. Remember what went on in your mind, in your heart, in your breathing, and in your stomach.

2. What environmental conditions existed to help you achieve the peak thinking experience?

3. What occurred, both mentally and physically, just prior to your peak thinking experience?

4. What conditions—either internally, externally, or both—would have to occur for you so that you could recall that peak thinking experience at any time?

Most clients find their responses to the previous questions very insightful. This is because they have taken an important step in bringing their unconscious thinking strategies into their conscious mind. Once a conscious awareness of their thinking strategies is established, they can further identify, clarify, and even refine them. The result is more peak thinking experiences that are available to them.

Examples of responses to the peak experience questions are provided below:

"I can relate overall peak thinking experiences to many particular instances, but the experiences themselves seemed similar as I thought about them.

Whether in business, family, or even in coaching the children's soccer or baseball team, the thought process heightened when I was motivated about the subject. I need to be excited about an end result. I need to feel good about myself and my surroundings—not trapped or pressured. I need to feel confident about the decision, good or bad. I feel quality thinking begins with feeling good about yourself. I have had times in my life when I have been at less than optimum physical shape and also been at marathon running condition. I believe my thinking and learning is at its peak when I am in above average physical condition. I think I am more confident about myself and it is reflected in my decision making. I also believe that when I am in that state I am under less stress or at least able to cope with stress more easily, and therefore able to have a sharper and more confident mind. I feel at times I have been in euphoric levels of thinking, where ideas flow more freely and I get excited about wider spans of topics. I truly believe, with a sharp body comes a sharp mind."

"A peak experience for me was when I generated the concept for the direction I wanted to take a particular show I was directing. I was able to determine the overall intention of the play by going into my quiet thinking mode. I chose to go to the library and get some reviews of the play and interviews of the author. I emphasize again that I am very visual and feeling. I read the reviews and interviews, got a sense of purpose, and then focused in on the fact that all the reviews mentioned family relationships. It was then just a matter of connecting the humor with the pathos. Being in the library and being surrounded by visual cues that expressed feeling and insight provided the positive environmental conditions for my peak thinking experience. Just prior to the peak thinking experience was the realization that I had all of the pieces I needed, I just needed to put them in order to fit the theme of humor. I needed to figure out how all of the emotions and ideas could be put in the context of humor. Once I figured it out, I was amazed that I hadn't seen it sooner, and I also marveled at the idea that once seeing it in a humorous context, I would be hard pressed to see it any other way. To recall that thinking experience again, I would have to be in a relatively quiet place so I could think, and I would have to keep in mind that I could make the pieces of the idea fit together by remembering that I have done it before very successfully."

Increasing our peak thinking experiences can be achieved through positive actions that are both stimulating and demanding. Here are a few examples of actions that we use to help achieve more peak thinking experiences:

Determine when and how our peak thinking experiences occur.

Maintain a positive attitude about our thinking abilities and believe in our ability to continuously improve and enhance our thinking.

Create a stimulating environment for ourselves—for example, display artwork, photos, play music, or adjust lighting and temperature in ways that help us think better.

Read a variety of articles, books, and stories. Then critically evaluate what we have
   read, or restate the central theme or idea in one or two sentences.

Listen to debates that occur on television and radio programs. Then critically evaluate both sides of the debates.

Observe how something works, and then develop a way to make it work better.

There are literally hundreds of ways to stimulate our thinking—the important point is to clarify what works for each one of us rather than rely solely
on trying to adapt what works for someone else. A useful technique has been
to have our clients develop a list of things that are likely to detract from peak
thinking experiences, and those activities they could do to continuously stimulate their thinking and achieve more peak thinking experiences. Also, we ask
them to think about the thinking process they used to come up with the
activities for the list and write down the characteristics of the processes.

Intelligence

When most people think about thinking, they can't help connecting it to
the term "intelligence." And unfortunately it is usually at that point when these
same people tell themselves they are not good at thinking because they do
not have (in their opinions) high intelligence. Their opinions couldn't be
further from the truth.

The last several decades have produced a significant amount of research
about the brain, the mind, and intelligence. The idea of representing intelligence simply by a quotient is not as prominent as it used to be, and that's
good news for all of us! In fact, Dr. Robert Sternberg contends that while the
IQ portion of a person's intelligence measures how well he or she does on
tests, the remaining portion of intelligence involves the person's ability to
learn from experiences and the levels of intuition and creativity he or she
applies to various situations.

Intelligence is commonly defined as the "capacity to learn or understand,"
or "capacity to acquire knowledge or understanding and then apply it in unique
ways." The key word to emphasize from both definitions is "capacity," which
in our opinion is something we all have available to us. So, even though we
may have scored a particular number in some intelligence test, the fact that
we have the capacity for learning, understanding, and applying concepts and
information means that our intelligence can continuously increase over time.

Over the years, several psychologists and others involved in the study of
human intelligence have proposed that intelligence is not isolated to a single
factor but rather to multiple factors. For example, Louis L. Thurston, a psychologist from the University of Chicago, believed that intelligence consisted
of seven "primary mental abilities." Thurston's seven factors included spatial visualization, perceptual speed, numerical, verbal comprehension, memory,
vocabulary, and inductive reasoning.[5] Psychologist J. P. Guilford developed

his structure-of-intellect (SOI) model, which describes intelligence in terms of a cube representing three intersecting dimensions of operations (mental processes such as memory and understanding), contents (various terms represented by words, numbers, or pictures that exist within a problem), and products (the types of required responses in terms of units, classes or relations). Guilford's theory proposes as many as one hundred and fifty factors within his SOI model.[6] Edward L. Thorndike hypothesized that intelligence within most people occurs as a result of structural bonds or connections that are formed between certain mental competencies. That is, performing a particular task is the result of these various connections being activated in ways that enable the task to be accomplished successfully.[7]

One of the most popular examples of multiple intelligences is from Dr. Howard Gardner, a Harvard psychologist, who has identified a model of intelligence based on seven intelligences that each of us possesses in varying degrees: (1) linguistic; (2) logical–mathematical; (3) spatial; (4) musical; (5) bodily–kinesthetic; (6) interpersonal; and (7) intrapersonal. We have found his approach very appealing to most people because it offers them a way to consider their complete potential in both learning and thinking styles. It also helps them appreciate the full potential of their intelligence rather than limiting their capabilities for intelligence to a numerical quotient.

When we apply the concept of multiple intelligences in our work with clients, we ask them to select from a list of intelligences the particular characteristics for which they consider themselves strongest. For example, some may classify themselves as having the characteristic of spatial intelligence because they are very sensitive to changes in their environment, have an excellent ability to accurately estimate sizes and dimensions, or enjoy mazes and jigsaw puzzles. In addition, these same people may also say they have a level of the social intelligence characteristic because they enjoy team projects and activities, like to socialize with others, and easily empathize with others. We also ask them to resist the temptation to categorize themselves into only one of the characteristics—each one of us is more complex than that. Most people find themselves described in several or sometimes all of the characteristics from our list. Together, these constitute their areas of strength, both in terms of thinking and personal learning style.

After developing their list, we ask clients to interpret what their selections might mean in terms of thinking and learning styles, preferred approaches to thinking, and environmental conditions that affect thinking. The following unfinished statements are used to help stimulate their interpretation of selections.

1. The most significant characteristics of my strongest intelligences tend to be_____.

2. My best time for thinking is likely to be_____.

3. My preferred approach for learning something new tends to be_____.

4. My preferred approach to developing a new idea or solving a new problem seems to be_____.

5. I mostly enjoy thinking in the following manner and environment_____.

Defining intelligence as the "capacity" to acquire knowledge or understanding, and emphasizing the concept of multiple intelligences from numerous psychologists, establishes a more positive mind-set for those with whom we work. Then, allowing them to select particular characteristics of various intelligences for which they consider themselves to be strong establishes tremendous insight that each person applies to his or her strategies for thinking.

SUMMARY

The power and functioning of the human brain is phenomenal, and there are particular portions of the brain that contribute to thinking. It is useful to understand and appreciate these portions of the brain and the fact that the brain's power can be increased. Learning and applying various exercises can enhance and strengthen our thinking skills.

Our experiences with learning have been the result of the particular educational system in which we participated. These experiences have contributed to how we think about our capabilities for better thinking. Revisiting and clarifying our experiences enables us to establish an understanding for how we think about learning, and the distinctions we make about learning and thinking.

NOTES

1. Pierce J. Howard, *The Owner's Manual for the Brain: Everyday Applications from Mind–Brain Research* (Austin, Tex.: Leornian Press, 1994), 266.

2. Roger B. Yepsen, Jr., *How to Boost Your Brain Power: Achieving Peak Intelligence, Memory and Creativity* (Avenel, N. J.: Wings Books, 1987), 101–102.

3. Robert J. Sternberg, *The Triarchic Mind: A New Theory of Human Intelligence* (New York: Viking Penguin, 1988), 75–76.

4. Abraham H. Maslow, *Toward a Psychology of Being*, 2d ed. (New York: Van Nostrand Reinhold, 1968).

5. Robert J. Sternberg, *Successful Intelligence: How Practical and Creative Intelligence Determine Success in Life* (New York: Simon & Schuster, 1996), 95–96, 97.

6. Martin A. Fischler and Oscar Firschein, *Intelligence: The Eye, The Brain, and The Computer* (Reading, Mass: Addison-Wesley, 1987), 7.

7. Howard Gardner, *Frames of Mind: The Theory of Multiple Intelligences* (New York: Basic Books, 1983).

Chapter Three

Thinking Processes and Strategies

Unconsciously, we apply particular strategies when we think. That is, we use particular methods to manage our thinking processes and achieve desired results. These particular methods are developed according to how we mentally process the signals from our senses. Then, these signals combine in a particular sequence to produce the thinking strategy we use to perceive and react to the conditions and situations encountered within various contexts. Identifying and formulating the specific strategies of our thinking processes enables us to consciously apply each strategy in various situations. Developing a conscious awareness of our thinking processes and strategies enables us to use and maximize them whenever and wherever desired.

THINKING STRATEGIES

Many people do not realize there are precise and unique strategies to their thinking—they think thinking just happens, and that it usually happens outside of their control. Some people believe that everyone's thinking is accomplished in the same way, except of course for the world's "highly intelligent" people, who must have some special gift.

Actually, our thinking is completely within our control and each of us has particular strategies that can be identified, applied, refined, and adapted to various situations. As human beings, we also have the ability to try out other people's strategies of thinking and apply them whenever we consider it necessary.

Nikola Tesla (1856–1943) was an American physicist and inventor who many consider to be the genius responsible for the age of electric power. Tesla was also one of the most creative inventors of the century, developing some seven hundred inventions, including the electromagnetic motor, turbine engine, and remote control devices. He had learned at a very early age that things and scenes he experienced would create vivid images in his mind. Often, though, he found it very difficult to "remove" his mental images. Rather than submitting to the unwanted images, he developed strategies for creating new images to take their place. Eventually, he further developed his visualizing capabilities by consciously creating new images and expanding the strength and clarity of his visions. He also discovered that the thoughts he had visually conceived were the result of external events. Recognizing this strategy, Tesla was able to use the external events to stimulate his curiosity about what inventions could improve the world around him. So, Tesla's awareness of his ability to create new visualizations from those that couldn't be removed, as well as the external events that stimulated visualized thoughts, enabled him to apply his thinking strategies to stimulate the development of inventions.

One of the most frequently reported examples of Albert Einstein's thinking strategies relates to his discovery of the theory of relativity. Einstein's thinking strategy was initiated by his curiosity about what the world might look like if he were sitting on the end of a light beam. From this curiosity, Einstein constructed visual images that represented his thoughts and made him aware of the muscular feelings he was experiencing during his visualization. He would fully associate himself into his visualizations so that he would see the images through his mind's eye. Finally, when he considered his visualization fully complete, he would translate the meaning of his images into words or mathematical symbols. In fact, in interviews, Einstein reported that he rarely began his thinking in the form of words or mathematical formulas. Rather, he used visual and muscular forms to create a deeper clarification and understanding of his curiosity so that he could then use words and symbols to represent his visualization. Einstein's thinking strategy consisted of combining his visual and feeling senses, which he then interpreted as particular words and symbols. For Einstein, this was an extremely productive method for achieving desired results.

The strategy of Walt Disney's thinking included three phases: visualizing, experiencing, and evaluating. Disney's creativity began by *visualizing* all of the various parts of a story or project, and mentally constructing a visual representation of the components from his own perspective. Next, he imagined himself actually *experiencing* the story (or the project, problem, or issue) from the point of view of the characters. In other words, he would put himself into the feelings of the characters and experience the event from their perspective. Finally, Disney took time reviewing and critically *evaluating* his creative work by visualizing its components in his mind. He did this by viewing his work from a perceptual position that was "above and farther away" than those created in the first two visualizations. Disney's thinking strategy enabled him to observe and test his creative ideas while they were still in his mind and before putting them on paper.

We have found that very few people have ever taken time to think about how they think, or to identify and clarify the "natural" thinking strategies they use. So the challenge is, how do we, as performance consultants, identify the thinking strategies of ourselves and others so we can help people apply those strategies consistently and think more productively? Responding to the challenge begins by expanding our awareness even further so that we can develop a detailed understanding of the strategies that form each of our thinking processes.

Up to this point, we have taken some preliminary steps in identifying and clarifying our thinking strategies. The questions from earlier exercises are helpful in stimulating our thinking about thinking. Our responses help us begin to discover some very useful information and enable us to gain some preliminary insight into our thinking preferences and strategies. It's really only the tip of the iceberg, though, and there is much more that we will discover.

THINKING PROCESSES

While each one of us has our own unique thinking strategies, there are also certain processes that all of us have in common. For example, we all tend to filter information coming into our brains, however, what and how we filter is determined by (1) the environmental conditions and events we are experiencing at the particular time; (2) our values, beliefs, expectations, and attitudes; and (3) our physiology and behaviors. The result of our filtering process is the creation of an internal representation, which in turn contributes to how we think about what we are experiencing. Also, we all take information in through any one, or a combination of, our senses; however, the particular senses we prefer to use to accomplish this process will contribute to our thinking strategies. Finally, we all have preferred patterns to our thinking, however, establishing and continuously applying those thinking patterns are based upon our unique and personal mental programs that operate our brain. Each of these processes contributes in a variety of ways to develop the thinking strategies we use on a regular basis.

Developing an awareness and understanding of our thinking strategies begins by understanding our thinking processes. These include the process of *filtering*, the process of *sensory linguistics*, the process of *internal sensory acquisition*, the process of *internal sensory modification*, and the process of *thinking patterns*. Each of these processes can contribute to the development and application of our thinking strategies in various contexts, provided we recognize and use them efficiently. For example, Nikola Tesla found his filtering process was one that would not easily delete images from his mind. Also, his internal sensory acquisition process was extremely powerful, particularly in terms of visualizations, and he used his internal sensory modification process to modify the images that could not be easily deleted. As a result of understanding his processes, Tesla was able to develop thinking strategies that enabled him to manage the processes. Each one of us can accomplish results similar to those achieved by Tesla, provided we are aware of our processes and apply thinking strategies to make those processes more efficient and productive.

Filtering

As human beings, we have a natural tendency to want to keep things simple for ourselves so we can quickly and efficiently process the tremendous amount of stimuli that constantly bombards us, particularly during our waking hours. Our brains use the process of filtering to help us make sense of the world around us, simplify our experiences, and represent information received through our senses. There are three components to our filtering process: deletion, distortion, and generalization.

Deletion helps us process a large amount of information without the need for every bit of detail associated with the information, and it occurs when we try to connect incoming visual or auditory information with what we already know. Our brains accomplish deletion by filtering out pieces of information or several parts of a total experience that we are encountering. Unfortunately, though, there are times when the filtering of information through deletion can cause us to overlook important details. For example, consider the situation where a person is driving a car through a busy intersection and sees the green light but deletes the pedestrian stepping off the curb and into the street. As a result of the person's rush to process a high volume of incoming information associated with driving, some very significant information is deleted.

An awareness of the deletion component is also important from the standpoint of objectively considering new ideas, improvements, and other forms of information. When we are presented with ideas and information that seem familiar to us, there is a strong tendency for our brains to quickly connect that information with similarly stored data and concepts. As a result, we may inadvertently think that we are familiar with new ideas or information being presented because of our brains attempt to delete what it considers to be similar details. While it is difficult, and even impractical, to expect ourselves to slow our brains down so as to consciously manage all details of an incoming message, we can encourage ourselves to take closer looks at what we might initially think are familiar ideas and information.

Distortion is used by our brains to change the perception of information and events that are actually occurring. As a result, it may add information that isn't there or edit details that do not match what is already known. When the brain cannot quickly recognize and classify incoming data, it adjusts or distorts that data for the purpose of creating some interpretation.

Unfortunately, because the brain rushes to classify and interpret new information and events, it often distorts it in ways that causes us to make interpretation errors. For example, consider the supervisor who observes an employee sitting back in a chair and staring at the ceiling. The supervisor will classify the meaning of that observation according to what is known from similar observations in the past. The supervisor may make an assumption that the employee is daydreaming rather than working, or make the assumption that the employee is taking time to contemplate solutions to a serious departmental problem. The meaning will depend upon how the supervisor's brain needs to distort the particular observation for classification and interpretation.

In order to effectively manage the filtering process of distortion, we need to be careful about how we allow our brains to distort and classify incoming data. We need to slow down our processing time so that we don't make an interpretation of information that isn't there or fail to classify and interpret information that is there.

Generalization occurs when we apply our learning and understanding from one context to another different context or situation. Very often, as a result of generalization, we tend to focus so strongly on applying our existing knowledge in a particular context that we fail to consider difference or alternative possibilities. For example, consider the person who receives bad service at a restaurant, and at a later date, when he finds out that a new restaurant in his neighborhood is owned by the same individual, he refuses to eat at the establishment. Carrying this example one step further, consider that he decides to try the new restaurant, but because his expectations are that he will receive poor service he tends to get what he expected. When our brains apply the filtering process of generalization, we tend to react to information and events according to certain expectations that we have established for ourselves. When we limit our expectations, we limit our full thinking capabilities. Therefore, it is useful to apply objectivity when dealing with situations of generalization and to recognize how our expectations can create undesirable self-fulfilling prophecies.

Sensory Linguistics

Each of us has particular preferences about how we use our brain to process the information that is received through our senses. Some of us prefer to process information visually, so we prefer that it be presented using words such as "see," "view," or "picture." Others of us prefer information be presented auditorily, so we find information to be more appealing when it is presented using terms like "hear," "listen," or "say." Still others think better when they get a feeling, a taste, or a smell about the information, and these people like information presented with words such as "grasp" or "handle" if they are feeling thinkers and "sweet," "sour," "scent," or "smell" if they are taste and smell thinkers.

We refer to the use of these preferences as the process of sensory linguistics because it pertains to how sensory-type words contribute to our thinking. That is, when information is presented using sensory-type words that match our preferred processing method, we find it much easier to accept and understand the information, and we are capable of processing the information more easily.

Determining our process for sensory linguistics, as well as that of others, can be accomplished by paying close attention to the words that are spoken, specifically the sensory-type words that are used. We then match the sensory-type words to improve information processing and thinking for ourselves and others. Consider the following examples.

Example 1: A salesperson is calling on a prospective customer. Let's assume that the salesperson uses a sensory linguistic process that is primarily visual while the customer's preferred sensory linguistic process is auditory. During the call, the salesperson describes his company, his products, and his capabilities in highly visual terms such as, "As you can *see* from our brochure_____," "Our customers *view* us as the leader in the industry_____," and "If you have a few minutes, I would be glad to *show* you_____." When the prospective customer provides information and answers the salesperson's questions, she uses auditory terms like, "People in production have been *telling* me they_____," "I've been *told* by my boss that_____," and "That just doesn't *sound* like it's right for us_____."

Throughout the call, the salesperson works very hard to clarify the customer's needs and requirements, and does a wonderful job explaining the features and benefits of his company's products, at least in his preferred terms. Unfortunately, the visual terms used by the salesperson do not match the customer's preferred sensory linguistic process that involves auditory terms. As a result, the salesperson leaves the call frustrated and wondering why the customer had a hard time understanding his presentation. The customer, on the other hand, wonders why the salesperson *showed* her all those brochures and charts when all she wanted him to do was *tell* her how his products would take care of the problems she has been *hearing* from the production people.

Example 2: A manager who uses a sensory linguistic process that is primarily auditory is interviewing a prospective employee whose preferred sensory linguistic process is feeling. During the interview, the manager describes the company, the work environment, and the job using auditory terms such as, "I'm sure you can *tell* from the job description that we need————," "Our employees *speak* very highly of the company because————," and "I've been *told* by others in the industry that our company————." When the prospective employee provides information and answers the manager's questions, he uses feeling terms like, "I have always *felt* that my employers have————," "My ability to *grasp* the meaning behind key business objectives————," and "Things *flow* smoothly for me————."

Throughout the interview, the prospective employee answers each and every question with the utmost sincerity, and is honest and forthright with his responses. Unfortunately, the feeling terms used by the prospective employee do not match the manager's preferred sensory linguistic process that involves auditory terms. As a result, the prospective employee leaves the interview feeling good about his responses but wondering why he didn't seem to make a positive impression on the manager. The manager, on the other hand, did not *hear* what she was hoping for from the prospective employee's responses. She's not exactly sure why, but the prospective employee's answers just didn't *sound* right to her.

Some examples of sensory-type words that pertain to our sensory linguistic process include the following:

Visual—see, picture, focus, view, clear, appears, looks like.

Auditory—listen, talk, hear, discuss, rings-a-bell.

Feeling—grasp, rough, handle, flow, smooth-over.

Taste—savor, sweet, spicy, tangy.

Smell—scent, get-a-whiff-of, breath-of-fresh-air.

Unspecified—think, understand, evaluate, consider, thought, know, believe.

The following examples illustrate how sensory-type words might be used in sentences.

Visual:

"Watch your life go by."

"I see what you are saying."

"That looks good."

"I'm hazy about that."

"I need to cast some light on the subject."

"I need to get a new perspective."

"I view it this way."

"Looking back on it now, it appears differently."

Auditory:

"This is a noisy restaurant."

"I hear what you're saying."

"That rings a bell."

"It sounds good to me."

"Everything just suddenly clicked."

"Listen to yourself."

"I've got this idea rattling around in my head."

"Something tells me to be careful."

Feeling:

"It just doesn't feel right to me."

"I can't get a handle on it."

"I finally grasped the concept."

"I need to get in touch with my feelings."

"I have a solid understanding."

"I'm up against a wall."

"I seem to get boxed in a corner."

Taste and Smell:

"The whole experience left a bad taste in my mouth."

"It just smells fishy to me."

"I'd like to take time to savor the moment."

"It's a sweet deal."

"That new system is like a breath-of-fresh-air."

The following activity is one that helps develop our awareness and use for the sensory linguistic process. During a five-day period, we make a concerted effort to listen for and use each one of the sensory-type words. For example, on Monday we listen for and primarily use visual words in conversations, on Tuesday we listen for and primarily use auditory words in conversations, and so on throughout the five days. We also focus our efforts on using the same type of sensory-type words that are being used by those with whom we are conversing. That is, even though it is the day we have chosen to emphasize visual terms, if a person we are speaking with uses auditory terms then we also use auditory terms in that particular conversation. Sometimes, too, depending on the situation, we may use the opposite sensory-type words than those being used simply to observe the reaction that the other person or persons have to the conversation.

Internal Sensory Acquisition

When we are asked to recall information, or when we think about some situation from the past or in the future, we go through a process of mentally acquiring that information. Internal sensory acquisition is accomplished by remembering or constructing the pictures, the sounds, and/or the feelings related to the information or experience. Neurological studies have determined that when the activation of various portions of the brain occurs, our eyes will move in corresponding vertical or horizontal directions. In other words, when thinking, we move our eyes in directions that correspond to whether we are acquiring information visually, auditorily, or through feelings at that particular moment in time.

The processes of internal sensory acquisition can be realized by watching eye movements. For example, if we were to create or recall some image or scene in our mind, our eyes would likely move up and to the right or left; if we were to create or recall moving images and scenes as if viewing a video, our eyes would likely be centered and looking straight ahead as though we were in a trance; if we were to create or recall sounds, our eyes would likely move horizontally either right or left; if we were to think about or recall feelings or bodily sensations our eyes would likely move down and to the right; if we were to have an internal dialogue with ourselves, our eyes would likely move down and to the left. These are examples based primarily on a right-handed person's eye movements. The eye movements will likely be reversed for the left-handed person. However, it is absolutely essential to consider these examples and the illustrations shown below as generalizations of the eye movements that occur as a result of internal sensory acquisition. Since each one of us is unique there will always be exceptions to our generalized examples. Therefore, in order to establish the meaning of our eye movements and those of others, it is necessary to establish the patterns that develop over time. For example, when we observe that a person's eyes move up and to the right each time he or she internally acquires a remembered visualization, then that is a pattern that provides a greater level of certainty about the meaning we place on the person's eye movements.

Figure 3.1 illustrates eye movements that typically result from the internal sensory acquisition process of a right-handed person. The location of the eyes in each illustration is meant to depict those of another person as we are looking at that person.

We help our clients practice the recognition and classification of internal sensory acquisition by having them read a series of questions or statements to another person and record the movement of that person's eyes in response to each one (that is, do the eyes go up, side-to-side, or down?). In our instructions, we tell clients that the other person should not be told that their eye movements are going to be observed because most people will then attempt to keep their eyes positioned in one place. We also instruct clients that each of the questions or statements must be presented clearly, precisely, and with appropriate emphasis to the other person. They should then pause several seconds between each question or statement. Finally, the person with whom they are working must respond to the questions or statements silently to themselves—they should not respond aloud.

Here are a few examples of the questions and statements that can be used to practice the internal sensory acquisition process:

"How many door knobs are in your place of residence?"

"What color is your bedroom?"

"Imagine a green dog on yellow grass."

"Who was the first person you saw today?"

"Where was the last place you signed your name?"

"How much is 570 x 3?"

"Picture a 747 jet with propellers on the wings."

Figure 3.1
Location of Eyes During Internal Sensory Acquisition

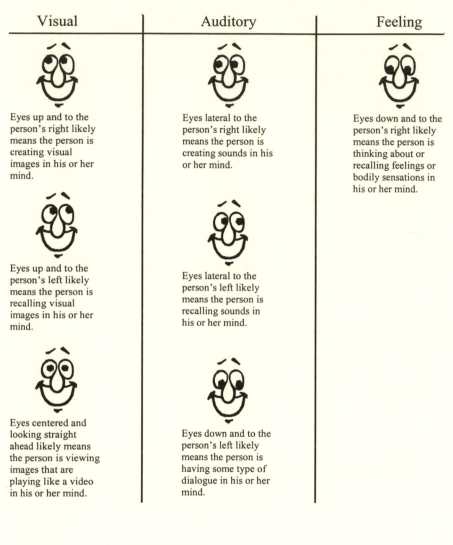

Visual	Auditory	Feeling
Eyes up and to the person's right likely means the person is creating visual images in his or her mind.	Eyes lateral to the person's right likely means the person is creating sounds in his or her mind.	Eyes down and to the person's right likely means the person is thinking about or recalling feelings or bodily sensations in his or her mind.
Eyes up and to the person's left likely means the person is recalling visual images in his or her mind.	Eyes lateral to the person's left likely means the person is recalling sounds in his or her mind.	
Eyes centered and looking straight ahead likely means the person is viewing images that are playing like a video in his or her mind.	Eyes down and to the person's left likely means the person is having some type of dialogue in his or her mind.	

"Hum a portion of your favorite song to yourself."

"Distinguish to yourself the sound of a door bell and a telephone ringing."

"What were some options that you had purchased on your last car?"

"Feel a snowball in your hands."

"Feel the heat of hot sand on your feet."

"How do you feel after eating a seven-course meal?"

"Think of the last time you had to slam on your brakes."

Internal Sensory Modification

Having acquired visual, auditory, or feeling information in our mind, we can discover that there are unique characteristics and fine distinctions to those images, sounds, and feelings. For example, consider the client who acquires a visualization of some remembered experience that she believes to be unpleasant. When asked to describe the visualization, the client tells us that she is seeing it through her own eyes, can see several people in it, the people appear much larger than she is, they are quickly moving in and out of focus, and the entire visualization is in black and white. When asked about the characteristics of a pleasant experience, she describes it as seeing herself in the picture which is panoramic, has vivid colors, and everything is bright and in focus. When the acquired information is auditory or feeling then the characteristics will be described accordingly, such as loud, soft, or with or without static, for sounds, and hot, cold, smooth, or heavy for feelings.

The internal sensory modification process then is that ability we have to modify, enhance, improve, or eliminate any or all portions of the information we acquire in our mind. It simply involves making desired adjustments to any of the images, sounds, or feelings that we have acquired so that we can recall them more quickly in various contexts, modify their levels of intensity to improve our reaction to them, and use them more efficiently for our thinking. For example, remember that Walt Disney evaluated his work by visualizing it "above and farther away" in his mind—one of the thinking strategies within his process of internal sensory modification. Understanding this thinking strategy enabled him to recall and use it for numerous creative projects.

This process is especially useful when helping clients distinguish between those situations when they consider their thinking to be either highly efficient or inefficient. Making them aware of the fact that they can identify precise differences between the two thinking experiences and then modify the internal representations of those experiences to increase the efficiency of their thinking is a powerful learning experience for many clients.

Some examples of how internal sensory information can be modified are provided in Table 3.1. To assist in the modification of the internal sensory information, many clients use a strategy in which they imagine their visual, auditory, or feeling characteristics to be connected to control knobs or switches similar to those found on a television set. Then, depending upon the characteristics that they want to modify, a control knob is used to make an adjustment in volume, brightness, intensity, color, texture, or clarity, or a control switch turns a characteristic on or off.

This is by no means an exhaustive list, and each distinction can be done in the opposite manner from what is listed. The point is to find the strategy that works best for each one of us and the results we want to accomplish for our thinking. We practice internal sensory modification by acquiring representations of different experiences in our minds and in various sensory forms.

Table 3.1
Internal Sensory Modification–Characteristics and Distinctions

Visual	Auditory	Feeling
Brightness: If dim, turn up brightness.	*Volume*: If loud, make softer.	*Intensity*: If strong, make weaker.
Focus: If blurry, sharpen clarity.	*Pitch*: If high, make lower.	*Size*: If large, make smaller.
Color: If black and white, add color.	*Tempo*: If fast, slow down.	*Temperature*: If hot, make colder.
Size: If images are too large, reduce their size.	*Location*: If close, make it far away.	*Texture*: If rough, make smoother.
View: If seeing through your mind's eye, view yourself in the visualization.	*Dimension*: If mono, make it stereo.	*Weight*: If heavy, make lighter.
Distance: If near, move away.		*Rigid*: If tight or firm, make flexible.
Movement: If fast, slow down or stop.		
Depth: If flat, make it 3-dimensional.		

We then modify the characteristics that pertain to each form to determine how the representation changes for us. For example, we might begin with a visual representation of an experience, then the auditory representation of the same experience, and then a feeling representation of the experience. Each time we modify the characteristics, we determine how the changes to various distinctions affect our thinking.

Thinking Patterns

Each of us uses particular patterns that affect our behaviors and thinking strategies. Our thinking patterns cause us to search for and evaluate information based on the perceived value of that information. As a result, the patterns we use to think about information contribute to the importance we place on that information and how it affects our thinking strategies.

Each one of us uses a variety of thinking patterns that are comfortable and make sense to us in various situations. The patterns we use relate to how we process and store information, and ultimately react to information either positively or negatively. The thinking patterns we use in particular contexts can be identified by listening for certain words and phrases, and being aware of certain actions that might be exhibited.

There are several thinking patterns that influence our strategies for thinking. They include *authority, similarity, precision, succession, credibility, activity, value,* and *believability.* A description of each pattern is provided on the following pages and shown as a continuum that ranges from one extreme to the other.

At one time or another and in one situation or another, we will use each thinking pattern at some level. Therefore, it is useful to consider where on each pattern's continuum we fall depending on a particular context. Also, it is important to reinforce the fact that none of the patterns are necessarily positive or negative, unless of course, we tend to overuse a certain one more than others. In those situations, we limit our flexibility and capabilities, and can often create undesirable reactions in others and ourselves.

Authority Pattern.   Our use of this pattern is based upon the sources of information and expertise, being either our "self" or "other" person, that we consider to have the greatest authority in a particular context.

When a person considers him or her "self" to be the authority, then the pattern is based on the person's own internal system of evaluation. The person is self motivated in a particular context, makes his or her own decisions, and knows internally the quality of his or her own work. In some contexts, the person may have some difficulty accepting the direction or opinions of others. The person who has a "self" authority pattern will have thinking strategies that respond to statements from other people such as "Only you know what is right," "The situation is up to you," or "Only you can decide."

When a person's authority and direction are based on the responses and opinions of other people, then the authority pattern is referred to as "others." This person will want to check with others about actions or decisions to be taken, and will want reassurance from others. The thinking strategies of this person respond to statements such as "Others would tell you the same thing I've told you," "The managers in other companies would tell you how important improved performance is to success," and "You know others have done the same thing." This person's thinking strategies also respond to specific testimonials from other sources.

Similarity Pattern.   This refers to the way in which we make comparisons about things and information as either being "identical" or "different."

When a person is motivated by and considers things and information based on the fact that they are "identical" to what is said and known, then that person is applying the "identical" pattern of similarity. This person's "identical" thinking strategies respond to statements such as "You will find that the idea I'm presenting is the same type that management has been considering for another facility," or "The type of program I'm recommending is just like the one that has been used successfully at your Northeastern branches." The "identical" thinking strategies would also respond to tangible items, materials, and information that are exactly the same.

The person who is motivated by and considers things and information according to how they are "different" from what is said and known applies the "different" pattern of similarity. He or she will often generate alternatives and exceptions by using the statement, "Yes, but . . ." This person's "different" thinking strategies respond to statements that generate alternatives, and he or she responds to tangible items, materials, and information that have clear differences.

Precision Pattern. This pattern relates to our preferences for different amounts of information, either "broad" or "exact," that are received and processed.

A person with a "broad" precision pattern needs to receive the overall concept of something (the big picture), rather than a lot of detail. For example, the person will talk in terms of the end result or bottom line without describing the details, and will likely be very capable of assembling something from a picture rather than the directions. The thinking strategies that the person uses within this pattern will involve moving directly to the conclusion or providing the desired end results.

The "exact" precision pattern is used by a person who needs to have all the details, and can have difficulty understanding the big picture if the details are not provided. For example, this person will want all the directions to assemble something. This person will use thinking strategies that involve getting all the details, including the people, places, and things, and the steps and sequences involved.

Succession Pattern. This involves our preference for using and receiving information or accomplishing activities in either "consecutive" or "random" manners.

The person who prefers the "consecutive" pattern likes to work within specific rules and procedures, and accomplish things in a very orderly and sequential manner. For example, many accountants will tend to use a "consecutive" pattern because accounting principles and procedures involve that type of approach. This person's "consecutive" thinking strategies involve information and events following or being in a precise sequence.

A "random" pattern of succession is preferred by the person who likes to do many things in different ways, and likes to have numerous options available. For example, the salesperson who prefers to set his own schedule and modify it at a moment's notice would likely be motivated by the "random" pattern. The "random" thinking strategies used by this person involve avoiding procedures while emphasizing the options that are available for accomplishing something and being capable of processing and using information that is received in an arbitrary way.

Credibility Pattern. This involves our preference for giving "credibility" to either what has occurred in the "past" or what will be in the "future."

The person who emphasizes what has occurred in the "past" has a preference for evidence from previous times and situations, and will also respond favorably to things that have been proven over time. For example, this type of person might buy the same model car because that model performed well over so many years. This person's "past" thinking strategies involve describing successes and results that *have been* accomplished over a previous period of time.

The person who emphasizes "future" is interested in what is possible, and is attracted to bigger risks that get greater returns. For example, he or she might buy stock in an unknown company because of a perceived potential for return. The "future" thinking strategies respond to descriptions about the *potential* for successes, and the results *that are likely to occur* over an upcoming period of time.

Activity Pattern. Our emphasis in this pattern is on "avoiding" problems to get to a desired result or "pursuing" specific actions that will achieve a desired result.

The person who achieves a desired result by being motivated to "avoid" the likely problems that would occur due to not achieving the result is using the "avoiding" activity pattern. For example, a person decides to improve his work habits because he wants to "avoid" being fired. The person's "avoiding" thinking strategies respond to information that describes the problems that can be avoided by achieving a particular result in some context.

The person who exhibits the "pursuing" activity pattern is highly motivated by the positive things that will occur from achieving desired results. For example, the CEO of some company implements a quality improvement process because he wants to achieve increased market share, higher profits, and greater quality of work life. The person's "pursuing" thinking strategies respond to descriptions of the positive results that can be achieved in certain contexts.

Value Pattern. This particular pattern pertains to the emphasis we place on either the "price" or "return on investment" of something.

The person who applies a "price" value pattern emphasizes the low cost of something in comparison to something similar that has a higher price. The "price" person uses thinking strategies that respond to information about the inexpensiveness and cost savings of one thing over another.

The "return on investment" value pattern is found in a person who may initially mention price yet prefers to pay a premium for something that will provide a significant return on his or her investment. This return on investment may be in dollars, but could also be in terms of time savings or high quality. The thinking strategies of the "return on investment" person respond positively to information that emphasizes how the price of something will be outweighed by related cost savings, improved efficiencies, increased productivity, or better quality.

Believability Pattern. This pattern involves the number of times we need to "see," "hear," or "feel" something (or any combination of the three) to be convinced. For example, some of us are convinced because "seeing is believing." Others of us are convinced of something through several "word of mouth" referrals. And still others of us need to "try something out" a few times before we are fully convinced.

The thinking strategies associated with the "see," "hear," or "feel" believ-ability pattern will react according to a person's preferred sensory stimulus and the number of times the stimulus must be presented. For example, a vice president of human resources for a large financial institution has a believ-ability pattern in which he is convinced only after he "hears" the proposed deliverables of a project three times and then "sees" the project deliverables presented in the form of a proposal.

Tracking Thinking Patterns

One of the best ways to develop an awareness and appreciation for the thinking patterns and strategies is to track their occurrences in various con-texts. To accomplish this, we use a simple tracking form that applies to each thinking pattern. We suggest that our clients record a brief description of the context in which they use a thinking pattern and then mark on the con-tinuum where they think they are related to the pattern. Then, they briefly describe the thinking strategy they used within the pattern.

Here's an example of how the tracking works. A client considers herself to have a "self" authority pattern in most contexts that involve purchases. How-ever, during the purchase of a computer she discovers that she uses a very high level of the "other" authority pattern because of the information she gathers from people and literature. She also determines that the thinking strategies she uses within this pattern are to talk with various people who she perceives as having knowledge about computers and software, and then review literature and other information to develop some knowledge about computers before making a purchase. Figure 3.2 is an example of the chart she completed.

Figure 3.2
An Example of an Authority Thinking Pattern Tracking Form

Description of Context: _Purchase of computer hardware and software_

Self _____ X____ Other

Description of Thinking Strategies Used: _Spoke with a friend who recently_
purchased a computer system and I got some great ideas on how to determine the
type of system I needed. I then went to two different computer stores and spoke
with several sales people who described the various systems and capabilities. I
obtained some literature about the systems I thought would be appropriate, read
through that material, and selected the system I wanted. Before purchasing the
system, I spoke with three more people who I knew and got opinions of my
proposed purchase.

The tracking form provides a useful way to identify and clarify our particular thinking patterns within various contexts. Remember that we all have the tendency to apply a certain level of each thinking pattern in particular contexts, so tracking which patterns we tend to use in each context is extremely useful to the awareness and development of our thinking strategies. An example of each thinking pattern's tracking form is shown in Figure 3.3.

SUMMARY

One of the most important objectives we have as performance consultants is to establish a conscious awareness of thinking strategies. Thinking doesn't just happen. There are precise and unique methods that each one of us uses to achieve desired results in certain contexts. Developing our ability as well as that of our clients to understand, identify, and apply those unique methods contributes to greater performance levels. There is nothing wrong with our thinking that some awareness and application won't improve.

Figure 3.3
Tracking Forms for Thinking Patterns

Authority Thinking Pattern

Description of Context: _____

Self _____ Other

Description of Thinking Strategies Used: _____

_____
_____
_____
_____

Similarity Thinking Pattern

Description of Context: _____

Identical _____ Different

Description of Thinking Strategies Used: _____

_____
_____
_____
_____

Figure 3.3 *(continued)*

Precision Thinking Pattern

Description of Context: _____

Broad _____ Exact

Description of Thinking Strategies Used: _____

_____

_____

_____

_____

Succession Thinking Pattern

Description of Context: _____

Consecutive _____ Random

Description of Thinking Strategies Used: _____

_____

_____

_____

_____

Credibility Thinking Pattern

Description of Context: _____

Past _____ Future

Description of Thinking Strategies Used: _____

_____

_____

_____

_____

Figure 3.3 *(continued)*

Activity Thinking Pattern

Description of Context: _____

Avoiding _____ Pursuing

Description of Thinking Strategies Used: _____

_____

_____

_____

_____

Value Thinking Pattern

Description of Context: _____

Price _____ Return on Investment

Description of Thinking Strategies Used: _____

_____

_____

_____

_____

Believability Thinking Pattern

Description of Context: _____

❏ See—number of times: _____   ❏ Hear—number of times: _____
❏ Feel—number of times: _____

Description of Thinking Strategies Used: _____

_____

_____

_____

Chapter Four

Process Models for Thinking

A review of literature pertaining to the topics of thinking and creativity contains numerous examples of models that represent thinking processes. These examples provide details of specific processes used to achieve desired results and make thinking a rewarding experience for the originator of the model. Process models are useful in determining particular stages within which characteristics of various thinking processes occur. Understanding the stages of a process model enables us to further clarify our own processes and related thinking strategies.

EXAMPLES OF PROCESS MODELS

Possibly the most widely applied model is the one used in *The Art of Thought*, written in 1926 by Graham Wallas.[1] He represented the creative thinking process with a four-step model that included *preparation* (the preliminary work of free-thinking, collecting, searching, listening, and allowing the mind to wander); *incubation* (the internal elaboration and organization of thoughts over a period of time); *illumination* (the recognition of insight or solution that is needed); and *verification* (critical assessment and acceptance of the insight or solution).

A Technique for Producing Ideas by James Webb Young lists five steps to his model.[2] First, gather raw materials (meaning those materials related to the issue or problem, as well as those related to our knowledge and experiences). Second, visualize and evaluate the materials in our mind. Third, allow our thoughts and ideas to incubate within our conscious and unconscious minds so that the "parts" form a useful whole. Fourth, give birth to the idea—the "Eureka!" state. Fifth, shape and develop the idea to make it useful.

How to Think Creatively, written in 1949 by Eliot Dole Hutchinson, describes four essential stages of insight that include *preparation* (the time, effort, and knowledge needed to fully clarify and understand some issue or problem); *frustration* (the "cessation of effort" for the sake of emotional balance and other activities); *insight* (a flood of ideas and alternative suggestions through the senses); and *verification* (the elaboration and evaluation of ideas and suggestions against realities).[3]

THE STRATEGIES FOR BETTER THINKING MODEL

Strategies for Better Thinking synthesize various models of thinking into four specific stages, as illustrated in Figure 4.1.

Figure 4.1
Strategies for Better Thinking Model

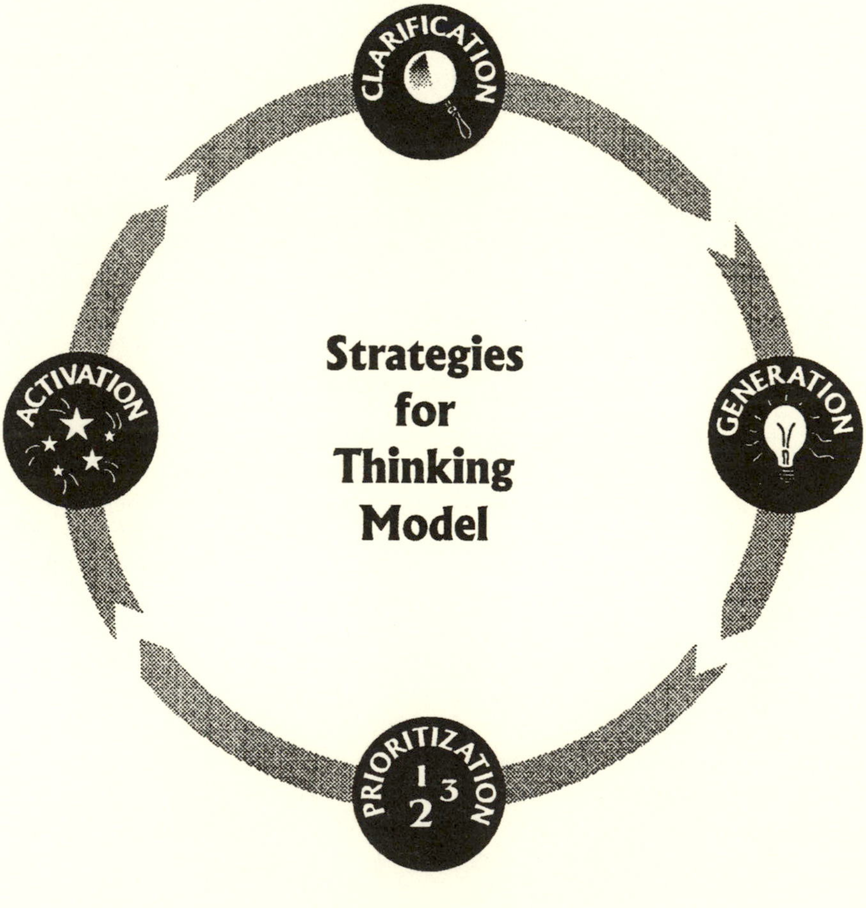

Some people wonder how the strategies for better thinking model is different from all those other models that illustrate approaches to thinking, creativity, problem solving, or other skills and concepts. At first glance, the difference may not be apparent. Like any other model, it is meant to serve as a representation or standard of excellence that can be imitated.

The real difference results from each person's application of the model. In other words, unlike other models that "force" a person into following its established steps, the strategies for better thinking model allows any person to use his or her existing thinking strategies within a proven series of actions. While other models tell us *what* to do, and to a limited extent how to do it, they rarely enable us to apply our own strategies. The power of the strategies for better thinking model is it helps us identify our thinking strategies within each stage, and then maximizes their use in various contexts. The characteristics of each stage of the model—clarification, generation, prioritization, and activation—are described below.

Clarification

The clarification stage prepares us for understanding what it is we want to think about, including desired outcomes and the positive and negative reactions to those outcomes. The purpose of this stage is to develop our awareness and appreciation for continuous improvements by focusing on the thinking strategies of perception, imagination, and intuition.

Perception involves the use of value judgments to immediately evaluate some thing or situation. Great thinkers apply thinking strategies that encourage the recognition of perceptions as neither accurate nor inaccurate, and promote the accurate interpretation of what has occurred rather than taking actions based only on the perceptions. The thinking strategies of perception can be practiced and enhanced by recognizing when we are perceiving and then taking steps to check what really exists. These thinking strategies can also be enhanced by presenting thoughts and statements in truly objective terms, while also evaluating value judgments to determine whether they pertain to what actually is at all times and in all contexts.

The clarification stage also includes the thinking strategy of imagination. Imagination is our ability to form mental images, create new ideas by combining previous experiences, or understand and apply others' creative resourcefulness. Imagination is best represented by children who experience everything in new and stimulating ways and who rarely place limitations on their ideas and thinking. Just as children do not apply the concept of expertise in their thinking, so too our imagination thinking strategies can be enhanced by avoiding the trap of expertise.

Imagination thinking strategies are developed through visualization and personal resource states. Various techniques can be learned and applied in order to enhance the art of visualizing. Personal resource states, which are our most positive mental attitudes that can be recalled when needed, establish a frame of mind that enhances our development, expansion, and continuous improvement of ideas. Personal resource states are developed through techniques such as association and dissociation, recognizing and modifying the characteristics of our internal states, and creating mental stimuli or signals that can elicit desired responses at any time.

The final thinking strategy within the clarification stage is intuition, which is our unexplained ability to know something without conscious reasoning. Intuitive thinking is based on some internal signals that let us know when to take action or when not to hold off from taking action. Great thinkers rely on a combination of intuition, reason, and logic to achieve greater levels of thinking and performance within the clarification stage. While there is no clear answer how intuition works, there are techniques that can be learned to help identify and apply our unique intuitive signals in various contexts.

Questioning techniques are also useful within the clarification stage because they develop a total and accurate understanding of some thing or situation. When constructed and presented well, questions enable us to expand our thinking by getting responses that come as close as possible to the actual meaning intended by others. This is possible through the application of specific questions as well as the use of at least two follow-up questions.

Generation Stage

The generation stage helps us identify and understand the strategies we use to creatively generate ideas and solutions, while also building the confidence and motivation needed to move toward achieving desired outcomes or avoid negative situations. Using the inventive genius of Thomas Edison and Yoshiro NakaMats as models for the generation stage, we emphasize the thinking strategies of information processing, connections, and motivation.

Information processing requires the application of practical techniques and thinking strategies that enable us to acquire and process data in ways that promote the generation of numerous ideas. While information processing is uniquely personal in style and character, we have found techniques that contribute to thinking strategies in this area. Internal techniques of information processing involve the acquisition, processing and analysis of information. External techniques of information processing involve the creation of environments that are conducive to our preferred organizational styles for idea generation.

Connections involve our ability to relate seemingly unrelated conditions or information, and as a result increase the generation of unique ideas. Our emphasis here is on a concept we refer to as linking, which can be developed through specific techniques and a lot of practice. Linking is a powerful thinking strategy that enables us to achieve more connections, thereby generating more ideas.

Motivational thinking causes, channels, and sustains our desire to generate ideas and then turn those ideas into reality. The thinking strategies associated with motivation are important for creativity and the generation of ideas because they increase our self-image and produce intense desire for achieving particular outcomes. Motivational thinking strategies are developed to a great extent by recognizing our needs in any given situation and at any given time. For example, we have found Abraham Maslow's hierarchy of needs model to be extremely useful for identifying thinking strategies within the categories of safety, security, social, esteem, and self-actualization.

The generation stage also includes a motivational technique we call reframing, which helps us think about information and situations in more than one way. Reframing generates thinking strategies that put new meaning around information or a situation, and thereby enhances our corresponding motivation.

Paradigm expansion is another important component of thinking strategies within the generation stage because it stimulates us to think beyond existing boundaries and the status quo. Greater levels of thinking and performance can be achieved by three actions of paradigm expansion that include (1) paradigm identification, (2) expansion of boundaries, and (3) expansion techniques.

Relaxation enables us to manage distractions, achieve greater levels of focus, and allow our conscious minds to settle down so the subconscious mind can get into action. Therefore, relaxation is an important component of the generation stage and the generation of creative ideas. Deep breathing, tensing and relaxing, and optimum environmental sourcing are three relaxation techniques applied within the generation stage.

Prioritization Stage

The prioritization stage enables us to put order into our thinking before moving onto the activation stage. That is, to consciously and unconsciously prioritize those ideas and solutions that were developed in the generation stage. Our strategies for prioritization are important because they enable us to focus on the most appropriate actions for particular contexts, while helping us objectively consider the priorities that are likely to bring about the greatest success and satisfaction. In other words, instead of using the same ideas and strategies in every context, prioritization allows us to determine the best ones for each situation.

We use top sales performers as a model for prioritization stage thinking strategies, and emphasize the thinking strategies they use to prioritize required actions. Top sales performers use thinking strategies that prioritize actions based upon importance and impact, what we call impact analysis. They determine the risk and value (impact) of their actions in relation to the results that need to be achieved. Impact analysis includes two methods: (1) the quick response method, which involves making quick decisions about the priority of activities and actions that are frequently encountered in a particular situation, and (2) the extended response method, which involves the prioritization of essential activities, such as long-range planning and research and development, that occur over an extended period of time.

Activation Stage

The activation stage focuses on thinking strategies that stifle action, as well as those that promote action. Both are important in certain contexts. For example, thinking strategies that promote low-level risk and stifle action may be most appropriate in some contexts, while those thinking strategies that promote greater risk and action may be best in other contexts.

The activation stage uses entrepreneurs as the model of action-oriented characteristics. The five categories of thinking strategies they use to promote action are identified and applied, including vision, congruence, self-reliance, decisiveness, and risk-taking. These categories not only help entrepreneurs prepare for taking action, they also enable them to test the actions for effectiveness and the likelihood of success.

SUMMARY

The strategies for better thinking model is a kind of road map that can be used on our journey to understanding, developing, and applying thinking strategies. Remember, though, that a road map provides many routes to the same destination, and our model is no different in that regard. There are many routes to achieving the thinking strategies presented within the stages of clarification, generation, prioritization, and activation. As performance consultants, we can select the route that is best in each context while helping our clients select those routes that are most useful to their situations.

NOTES

1. Graham Wallas, *The Art of Thought* (New York: Harcourt, 1926).

2. James Webb Young, *A Technique for Producing Ideas* (Chicago: Advertising Publications, Inc., 1951).

3. Eliot Dole Hutchinson, *How to Think Creatively* (New York: Abingdon-Cokesbury Press, 1948), 38–40.

Chapter Five

Clarification Stage

Where does one's thinking start? How does one come up with that great idea? Before Disney dreamed of a story by visualizing all the elements, and before Einstein constructed images and feelings that represented his thoughts, each had clarified a desired outcome to be achieved. Their thinking went beyond what currently existed, beyond the status quo, and beyond their contentment with various aspects of their life. They wanted something more than what was available to them.

To emphasize this point and illustrate the importance of the clarification stage, consider the following quotations.

"Discontent is the first step of progress. Show me a satisfied man, and I will show you a failure." Thomas Alva Edison (1847–1931), American inventor.

"A wise man will make more opportunities than he finds." Francis Bacon (1561–1626), Lord Chancellor of England.

"The reasonable man adapts himself to the world; the unreasonable one persists in trying to adapt the world to himself. Therefore, progress depends on the unreasonable man." George Bernard Shaw (1856–1950), Nobel Laureate in literature, *Man and Superman.*

"The people who get on in this world are the people who get up and look for the circumstances they want, and, if they can't find them, make them." George Bernard Shaw, *Mrs. Warren's Profession.*

Each one of the quotations emphasizes the importance of one's awareness and appreciation for making continuous improvements. This is the primary purpose for the clarification stage of thinking. If a person goes through life telling himself that he is thoroughly content with the way things are, or failing to achieve greater opportunities for himself, his family, his company, or society, the chances of being perceived as a great thinker (or even a mediocre thinker) are very slim.

We do acknowledge that many people react to this as being much easier said than done. And for some of them, it probably is. There are no simple formulas that can be provided. But that does not mean we can't develop our natural abilities for spotting and clarifying important trends and improvements in our lives.

CLARIFICATION STAGE: PERCEPTION, IMAGINATION, AND INTUITION

Achieving the benefits of the clarification stage involves awareness and development of three important capabilities: *perception, imagination,* and *intuition* (not necessarily in that order).

Perception

How does a person perceive some thing or situation? Most people respond to that question with something like, "I see it and then make some interpretation about it." While that answer is correct for many of us, perception is actually much more than the two components of seeing and interpreting.

People will not only "see it," but very often hear, touch, taste, and/or smell it as well. People will not simply make an "interpretation about it," but will respond to various verbal and nonverbal cues; make value judgments about the thing or situation based upon past experiences; form mental impressions about their judgments; and respond in some way either consciously or unconsciously.

Individuals considered great thinkers accomplish "perception" with one slight exception—they do not immediately evaluate the thing or situation with a value judgment. Rather, they recognize that perceptions are neither accurate nor inaccurate, and that the meaning behind a perception must be interpreted and understood before taking some action. In other words, the proper response to a perception is based on accurately interpreting what has occurred rather than acting only on the perception of what occurred—they check out their perceptions.

It is not only useful to understand what great thinkers do to accurately perceive experiences, but also what they do not do. Like great thinkers, we can improve the interpretation of our perceptions by avoiding the following natural tendencies.

Avoid being influenced by subliminal cues or our familiarity of things in particular contexts. A person dressed in old blue jeans, black boots, and a leather jacket, and driving a Harley-Davidson motorcycle is not necessarily a member of Hell's Angels.

Do not interpret the cues from one person based on how we have defined similar cues in the past. A frown can mean many different things on people.

Do not respond to cues that are not directly related to the current context. Clothes are not an accurate representation of personality or competence.

Do not let emotions get in the way of a rational and accurate interpretation of an experience. Liking a particular speaker doesn't make his or her message accurate.

Avoid being positively or negatively influenced by sources considered to be experts. Just because a professor says that the overnight shipment of packages through Memphis, Tennessee is not possible doesn't mean it's true.

Do not act on our perceptions without knowing all the factors that influenced them. Unfortunately, many people consider only one or two factors when acting on their perceptions. What are the factors influencing perception of this book?

Perception Exercises. Great thinkers put a lot of effort into responding objectively to their perceptions rather than subjectively. So, to enhance the perception portion of the clarification stage, we use the following exercises. Take some time to work through each one yourself.

Exercise 1: In the space below, write at least five statements that describe a coconut. Be sure to put the statements in objective terms.

Now, go back and review the statements. How many are actually objective? For example, some people will include a statement that coconuts are round, when in fact some coconuts are not completely round but are variations of round. Go back to your statements and evaluate their objectivity.

Exercise 2: Think of a person you know. For example, your spouse, your boss, a team member, or anyone for whom you can list at least five objective statements to describe how you perceive the person.

Now, go back and determine if the statements are truly objective. For example, "he is more than forty years old," is an objective statement. "He is ambitious," is a subjective statement or value judgment. If any statements are value judgments, then perceiving is being made subjectively rather than objectively.

Our perception of someone or something will change dramatically when we stop evaluating, or making value judgments, and think about *what actually is* versus *what might be.*

Here's a good way to check the value judgment of statements. After each statement, ask the following question: "Have I made a statement about what actually is, at all times and in all contexts, or have I made a statement that only represents my perception?" Now, go back and change value judgment statements to ones that are objective.

Now, consider the following situation, you notice a friend walking down the street, you wave at your friend, but your friend does not respond to you. What value judgments do you make?

Your judgments may or may not be correct. To find out, you need to check with your friend to determine which of your judgments are and are not correct.

Exercise 3: Consider the example in Figure 5.1. What is your perception of the vertical lines?

Many people's perception of the vertical lines above is that the left line is longer than the right. Do we just accept what our mind sees or will we check it out? How will we check it out?

Here's another example. In Figure 5.2, does line A connect with C or does line B connect with C? How would we check it out?

Figure 5.1

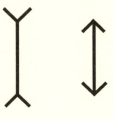

Figure 5.2

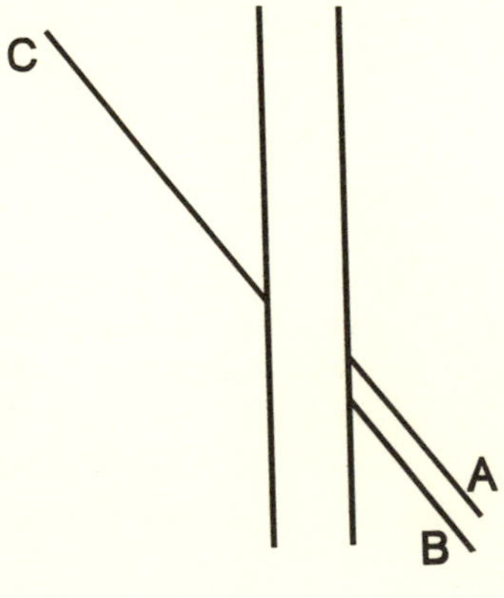

Here's another example. In Figure 5.3, which center circle is larger, the one on the left or the one on the right? How would we check it out?

The point of the previous examples is that our perceptions can be deceiving if they are not checked against what really exists. Great thinkers tend to recognize when they are perceiving something, and then take necessary steps to check their perceptions with what really exists.

Additional methods we use to illustrate the issue of perception are described in Exercise 4 and Exercise 5.

Exercise 4: Choose a blank wall. Stand about five feet back. Close your eyes and inch your way very slowly toward the wall. When you "perceive" that you are an inch from the wall open your eyes and discover the accuracy of your perception.

Exercise 5: Increase your perception of time by sitting quietly and determining when you think three minutes have expired. This is done without counting or looking at your watch.

Imagination

The second characteristic within the clarification stage is imagination. In terms of definition, imagination is the ability to form mental images of what is not present, the ability to create new ideas by combining previous experiences, or the ability to understand the imaginative creation of others' resourcefulness.

Consider the imagination of a child. For a child, everything encountered is new. There are no rules per se, and a child can make a game out of any thing or situation. Children are naturally creative because, unlike many of their adult counterparts, they do not place limitations on their ideas or thinking. For example, as soon as we proclaim ourselves as "experts" in something, we have begun to limit our imagination. Too many years in a particular field can keep an individual from pursuing the excitement and initiative of finding new and

Figure 5.3

better ways of doing things within that field of expertise. Success or expertise can become a serious enemy to our natural thinking strategies.

If we reach a point where we accept all the conclusions from our expertise then we are in danger of stifling our thinking and the clarification stage. Great thinkers continually go beyond what has been, and develop new ideas for what is possible.

The imagination capability within the clarification stage can be enhanced by avoiding the trap of expertise. The following suggestions have helped us maintain our imagination.

Be open to ideas from others who are not directly involved in our area of expertise. They will have open minds and fresh perspectives that offer new approaches. This is due primarily to the fact that experts have established particular paradigms from which escape can be difficult. On the other hand, a newcomer to a field of expertise is not locked into any paradigm and can offer new perspectives without preconceived notions.

Don't complicate ideas or solutions. When we consider a great thinker's imagination, our awe often results from the fact that they came up with an idea that was so "simple." The simple ideas are all around us, but they can only be grasped when we are not locked into the paradigms of our expertise, or one way of doing things.

Expose ourselves to information and ideas, particularly information and ideas that come from sources outside our expertise.

Do things differently from the way we are used to doing them. For example, if we tend to do things randomly, we do some consecutively; if we tend to do things consecutively, we do some randomly.

Industries are filled with experts who have failed to use their imagination to expand not only their industries but also their businesses as well. For example, consider the following—wouldn't it have been logical for Kodak to have invented a Polaroid-type film? What kept watch makers from inventing digital watches?

Frank Lloyd Wright once defined an expert as "A man who has stopped thinking." There are numerous examples from virtually any public and private organization where experts failed to use imagination to expand their fields of specialty or business.

Another part of imagination is being able to take advantage of those flashes of insight that develop at the most inappropriate or unexpected times. Very often, the greatest ideas and most creative thoughts come to us when we are not consciously trying to develop them. As Louis Pasteur observed, "Chance favors the prepared mind."

Great thinkers increase their ability to be prepared and increase their imagination by doing the following:

Expose themselves to extensive information.

Make connections between their areas of expertise and those of other industries and areas of expertise.

Connect seemingly unrelated events or items to their area of investigation.

Think in terms of new and continuous improvement.

Remain motivated, dedicated, and determined to achieve their desired outcomes.

Continuously familiarize themselves with nature and other things in their environment.

Continuously develop their senses, particularly the ability to visualize.

Imagination through Visualization. The imagination of many great thinkers occurs in very vivid visual form. Here are a few examples:

Albert Einstein would physically associate himself into the imaginary thoughts he constructed, as he did when he imagined what the world would look like if he was sitting on the end of a light beam.

Nikola Tesla was known as a visionary futurist and has been called "the genius who ushered in the power age." He would make what he called "excursions beyond the limits of the small world" and visualize himself living in the imagined time.

Elias Howe solved his problem by inventing the sewing machine when he visualized the image of a needle with the eye in the point.

Each one of us can maximize our natural thinking strategies by learning and applying the visual and other mental strategies of great thinkers. Many of us already use and apply similar strategies in our everyday lives, while others have the strategies but either are unaware of the capabilities or have not perfected their use.

Since much of imagination is visual, we have found it useful to develop and perfect our visual strategies and capabilities with the following exercises.

Exercise 1: This exercise is used to help construct visual imagery.

Find a comfortable position for yourself. Close your eyes and take three slow and deep breaths. Imagine the area around you is painted with your favorite color.

Continue to breathe slow and deep, and as you do, begin to feel your entire body relaxing from your toes and running completely through your body to the top of your head.

Take a couple of moments to enjoy this relaxation and the color that surrounds you. Say to yourself, "I like my surrounding area and can visualize it clearly."

Now, on your colored surrounding area, begin to visualize something you like very much—a favorite person, place, or thing. If you need to, slowly bring the image into focus as much as you can. Say to yourself, "I can make this image as focused as I like."

Begin to see or sense the details of your visualization. Is it in focus or out of focus? Is it in color or black and white? Is it still or moving? Are there sounds, feelings, or smells associated with the image? Does the image change when sounds, feelings, or smells are added to it? Do you see yourself in the visualization or are you seeing it "through your own eyes?"

Allow the image to slowly fade away so that the colored surrounding area is all you see. Take a few moments to continue to breathe slowly and deeply, and enjoy the relaxation you feel. Recall the experiences that occurred for you during the visualization.

When you're ready, open your eyes and congratulate yourself for the results you achieved in the exercise. Take a few moments to write down the details of your visualization experience.

Like anything else in life, visualizing comes easily for some and is difficult for others. Fortunately, there are methods that can be used to develop and enhance one's visualization capabilities. Consider the following examples.

Change physiology. For example, stand rather than sit; sit rather than lay down; put head back rather than forward; or look up rather than look down.

Identify the thoughts and experiences that bring about a visualization easily and naturally, such as a favorite person, place, or thing. Start with these images, adjust their strength and clarity, and then bring other images into the visualization.

Start with a small segment of a larger visualization or break a larger visualization into smaller segments.

Reduce or eliminate internal and external interference, such as a critical internal voice or external sounds and images.

Connect the visualization to other senses that may be more dominant. For example, if a person has a strong auditory sense, we suggest beginning with a favorite song or saying and connect some image to it. If a person has a stronger sense of feeling, we suggest he or she starts by remembering something that gave a positive feeling and then develop a visualization that represents the feeling.

Exercise 2: The following exercise is useful for practicing the ability to construct future visual imagery. Try this exercise yourself by asking someone to read the steps to you.

Think of something you want to accomplish in the future. It might be an idea you want to implement, a problem you want to solve, a presentation you want to give, or a project you want to complete.

Find a comfortable position for yourself. Close your eyes and take three slow and deep breaths.

Imagine the completion date of the thing you have selected. Then, determine the location, people, and any other details you think are related to the future visualization.

Continue to breathe slow and deep, and as you do begin to feel your entire body relaxing from your toes and running completely through your body to the top of your head.

Take a couple of moments to enjoy this relaxation and begin to formulate the components and characteristics of your visualization. Say to yourself, "I like this future and can visualize it clearly."

Now, begin to visualize the various aspects of your completed future. For example, visualize what your completed idea looks like and what it is like with your problem solved. Take time to imagine the details of how you successfully got to this future time. If you need to, slowly bring the various aspects of your future visualization into focus as much as you can. Say to yourself, "I can make this visualization as focused as I like, and I know what I did to achieve this future."

Allow your visualization to slowly fade away and begin to visualize yourself back at the present date, time, and location. Continue to breathe slowly and deeply, and enjoy the relaxation you feel.

When you're ready, open your eyes and congratulate yourself for the results you achieved in the exercise. Take a few moments to write down the details of your visualization experience.

Imagination through Personal Resource States. Another aspect of imagination is putting ourselves in a frame of mind that allows us to develop, expand, and continuously improve our ideas. For some of us, ideas come at the most inappropriate times—that is, not when we are trying to think of them, but rather when we are relaxed and allow our thoughts and imaginations to flow freely through our minds.

Developing a personal resource state for generating ideas greatly enhances our ability to quickly relax and maximize the flow of our imagination. There are several important concepts to understand when creating our resource states. First, making a distinction between *association* and *dissociation* is important, as is the ability to switch between *associated* and *dissociated states*. For example, an associated state is when we are seeing a visualization through our mind's eye (living it), and a dissociated state is when we are seeing ourselves in a visualization (watching it). Second, recognizing and modifying the *characteristics of our internal state* is important. An example of this is changing the characteristics of a negative internal sound or voice to characteristics that are considered more positive. Third, *creating a mental stimulus*—a signal, like some reminder or symbol, that elicits a particular response that we can stabilize and then recall is important as well.

Association and Dissociation. Association refers to being fully in the experience and having the feelings, sights, and sounds of the experience. Dissociation refers to being disengaged, outside of an experience, and separated temporally or spatially, or by being only aware of one part and not one, or a number of other parts. Both association and dissociation are useful and have certain advantages. Also, there are specific techniques that can be used to achieve each one.

Association enables us to access a resource state, allows us to rehearse some behavior or activity, and enables us to fully access and "be in" an experience. To be associated, we mentally visualize an experience through our own eyes, pretend "as if" we are experiencing a behavior or activity, and create an experience in the moment.

Dissociation enables us to view a situation more objectively and gain a new perspective, allows us to objectively evaluate or assess a situation, allows us to separate ourselves from overwhelming feelings or pain, and enables us to take on different roles and access feelings, and/or opinions. To be dissociated, we mentally visualize an experience from outside our body—for example, seeing ourselves in the situation, pretending we are younger, older, and/or in a certain setting, or mentally visualizing ourselves above a situation as it is occurring.

Have someone read the following narratives to help you experience the difference between an associated and dissociated state.

Make a picture of yourself on a roller coaster—as if you're watching a movie of yourself. See yourself in the first seat going up that first big hill and watch the car climb slowly up the hill. Watch, as the car tips over the hump and you see the roller coaster car with you in the first seat speeding down the track—you see your hair blowing—you see excitement on your face—and you hear the screams coming from your mouth. Now, as the roller coaster car dips up from the bottom of the run and starts up again, enter your own body so that you can feel yourself sitting in that first seat. You look up and see the greasy chain pulling you toward the top of the next hill—you hear the clanking of that chain—and you now feel the car pulling you higher and higher toward that peak. As you reach the peak, you can see all the way out and down—you see your hands gripping the car's hand rail. And as the car suddenly dips down the hill you feel the wind against your face—you feel your stomach rise as your body drops—and you hear your own screams as you race toward the bottom.

Obviously there is a big difference between the two experiences. That difference is crucial. When we are watching ourselves, as on a movie screen, seeing ourselves in the picture, we are in a dissociated state. As such, we are not directly experiencing the feelings, sounds, and sights that are an integral part of the situation. The opposite is true when we are associated into the experience.

Developing our application of association and dissociation requires practice. The following three-step exercise can help achieve that practice.

Step 1: Think of some experience involving a successful idea from the past, and remember it as you originally saw it, heard it, and felt it.

Become aware of your reactions and other aspects of the experience, such as feelings, or mental images, and if it is associated or dissociated. Whichever it is, think of it again in the opposite manner.

Was it remembered the first time in an associated or dissociated manner? How did changing the remembered experience change the effect of the experience?

Step 2: Think of the same experience, and view it from a future perspective (for example, explaining it to a grandchild). Notice the internal and external reactions to this experience in an associated and dissociated manner.

How did thinking of the experience in a future associated manner change the effect of the experience? How did thinking of the experience in a future dissociated manner change the effect of the experience?

Step 3: Write down the differences and similarities of each experience.

Characteristics of Our Internal State.   Recognizing and modifying the characteristics of our internal state relates to the internal sensory modification section of Chapter 3. The characteristics of our internal state include the fine distinctions pertaining to the visual, auditory, and feeling conditions that develop when we process information and activate our imagination. It is useful to go back and review Table 3.1, *Internal Sensory Modification—Characteristics and Distinctions,* before accomplishing the following two-step exercise. We use this exercise to help clients get a sense of how internal states change between positive and negative experiences. It also helps them practice identifying, describing, and modifying their internal sensory characteristics that apply to their thinking strategies. The two steps described below are worded in the manner that we state them to our clients.

Step 1: Think of a positive experience involving a successful idea from the past. It could be the same experience used in the previous exercise. Then, "step in" and "step out" of the experience and identify how the visual distinctions, auditory distinctions, and feeling distinctions change each time. Also, identify and describe how your internal state changes each time.

Step 2: Now, think of the same experience using different visual, auditory, and feeling distinctions. For example, if you had visualized the experience in color, try it now in black and white. Do these changes in the distinctions also change your internal state? How exactly does your internal state change? Which distinctions provide you with the greatest thinking state?

Creating a Mental Stimulus for Imagination—Signaling.   A mental stimulus, which is a personal *signal,* is some reminder or symbol that elicits a particular response which we can stabilize and then recall whenever we need it.

The technique of signaling can be used to deliberately create the conditioned response from some stimulus. A signal is established using words, visuals, or touch (which represent the stimulus) while a person is fully associated in a present or past experience. Then, when the stimulus is repeated by our signaling, the response will again occur. For example, have you ever heard a favorite song, and remembered the time when you gave it a special meaning? When you heard the song, were you able to see the situation, hear the sounds associated with the situation, and even have certain feelings about the experience? That song is a "signal" for you.

There are five conditions that are important when creating a mental stimulus or personal signal. They include occasion, duration, characterization, location, and duplication. Occasion refers to *the timing* of when the signal is set. The best occasion for a signal is just before and just during the peak experience of the person. Duration refers to *the length of time* needed to set the signal. Typically, the signal must be held for at least five seconds and ideally until the person is totally in the experience. Characterization refers to *the kind of stimulus* used to create a signal. The uniqueness of the stimulus is very important because it will more precisely trigger the response. Location refers primarily to *the placement* of feeling signals, but can also pertain to the location of visual and auditory signals. Duplication refers to the *recreation* of a signal to increase its intensity. The stimulus of the signal must be precise and easily repeated.

Signaling helps us identify and develop personal resource states that enable us to activate our imagination and ideas whenever we wish. We use the following two-step exercise to teach clients how to create mental stimuli through the technique of signaling.

Step 1: Identify and describe a resource state that has enabled you to come up with ideas quickly and easily. Also, determine the context in which you want this resource. For example, you might want the resource when working with an important customer. Think of the context in positive ways and state it in positive language. Then, decide on the visual, auditory, or feeling characterization you want to use for the signal, and also its location.

Now, think of a time when you fully, intensely, and congruently experienced the state. Then, associate into that state.

As you go into the peak of the experience, set the signal and hold it during the entire time that you recall the experience in your mind.

Release the signal, and then break the state by saying out loud, "I'm back in the present and feeling great."

Test your signal by thinking of a context and time in the future when you will need the signal to bring about the resource state. As you think of this future situation, test your signal and check the change in your state.

Step 2: Now that you know how to create a mental stimulus by setting a signal for yourself, practice by creating several additional signals for other contexts where you want to be at a peak thinking experience. Use the procedure from Step 1 as a guide.

Intuition

Intuition is probably one of the most fascinating characteristics of great thinkers. Intuition is that unexplained ability to know something without conscious reasoning—for example, to "just know" what the right course of action should be, what the latest business trend is that will develop, or what needs to happen to bring an idea into being.

Intuition is the immediate knowing that occurs without any apparent connection to reason and logic. For some of us, the idea of intuition is either ignored or explained as accidental or random in its occurrence. Unfortunately, this attitude can dramatically reduce our ability to take advantage of the natural capacity for intuitive thought. Great thinkers rely on intuition as the internal sense that helps them get the most out of reason and logic.

Consider the following illustrations of intuition:

Illustration 1: You've been offered a very desirable position with a relatively new, yet apparently very successful, organization. The organization has an extensive list of national accounts, has a good reputation among others in its industry, and has an energetic group of employees. While thinking over the offer you've been presented, your internal signals tell you to wait with any firm decision. You inform the organization's management that you will not be available to accept the position for at least six months. Within three months, the organization is out of business.

Illustration 2: You return home from work and discover you do not have your reading glasses. You remember using them in the meeting you attended before leaving work. You get back in your car to return to the office. Before you back out of your driveway you impulsively reach under the front seat and discover your glasses on the floor.

We have found the previous stories to be similar to ones that many others have experienced, or they remind people of other situations in which their intuition paid off for them. After sharing these and other illustrations with clients, we ask them (1) what came to mind as you heard us read the situations? and (2) what intuitive experiences have you had? We then ask them to record a situation where intuition worked for them by recalling the sights, sounds, and feelings associated with the intuitive experience.

So how does intuition work? Unfortunately, there is no clear answer. When intuition strikes, it gives us the ability to "just know" what to do. This makes the process of intuition difficult to understand because the knowing is not based on reports, studies, charts, or other tangible sources of information. Rather, intuition is based on some internal signals that make us "just do it," or "hold off on doing it."

In his book *The Luck Factor*, Max Gunther describes the "hunching skill" which illustrates the connection between intuition and tangible data.[1] "A hunch is a conclusion that is based on perfectly real data or objective facts that have been accurately observed, efficiently sorted, logically processed in your mind. The facts on which the hunch is based however are facts you don't consciously know. They are stored and processed on some level of awareness just below or behind the conscious level. This is why a hunch comes with that peculiar feeling of almost—but not quite—knowing. It is something that you think you know but you don't know how you know it."

Some of the best decisions in life are not based on available data. Very often, if not always, a decision is developed from intuition, and as Max Gunther's quote states, from information that is already stored unconsciously, which in turn creates the feeling about moving or not moving on a particular decision. It is a sensing of what is right.

Since everyone's internal intuitive signals are unique, a specific process of intuition cannot be taught. However, we can learn to identify our intuitive signals. Then, once identified, we can practice recognizing the signals and putting them to use in various contexts. For example, think of an experience in which your intuition resulted in something positive for you. Fully describe the experience and provide as much detail as possible about what exactly happened—both internally and externally.

There are several characteristics of an intuitive experience:

It occurs spontaneously—when it is least expected.

It can't be made to happen; it has to be recognized when it happens.

It can be enhanced through relaxation, patience, humility, and self-control.

It is very different from hope or desire and from emotion or intellect.

It can be developed by clarifying the distinctions and patterns that exist when it occurs.

It gives the sensation of being certain about something—we know when we've experienced it.

It augments the logical and hard facts, and makes us conscious of the soft facts in a situation—things like impressions, feelings, and inclinations.

It is typically experienced when choices need to be made, and signals a go–no-go response.

There are specific actions we can take to help us increase our intuitive abilities. The actions include the following:

Use relaxation techniques to calm our minds.

Identify and maintain a state of flexibility and objectivity.

Accept our hunches.

Stimulate ideas through techniques such as brainstorming, mind mapping, writing, and drawing.

Take risks—to paraphrase Anthony Robbins, "There are no failures, only results."[2]

Expand our existing paradigms.

Develop an awareness for what happens (what we see, hear, feel, taste, and smell) when our intuition is correct.

Focus on something other than the issue or problem we want to solve.

Don't force ourselves to be intuitive—it will resist.

Have faith and confidence in ourselves and our abilities.

We have found it possible to identify and clarify our internal signals that relate to either positive or less than positive intuitive experiences. We use the following exercise to help ourselves and our clients practice this. Try these exercises for yourself.

Exercise 1: Find a comfortable position for yourself. Close your eyes and take three slow and deep breaths.

Recall a positive intuitive experience. Include the location, people, and any other related details.

Continue to breathe slow and deep, and as you do, begin to feel your entire body relaxing from your toes and running completely through your body to the top of your head.

Take a couple of moments to enjoy this relaxation and begin to recognize the complete details and characteristics of your intuitive experience. Also, clarify the sequence in which these characteristics occur. For example, if your intuition was a visualization, what was its characteristics and in what order did they occur? If it was a combination of visual, auditory, and/or feeling characteristics, what were they and in what order did they occur?

Take time to imagine the details of your successful intuitive experience. Because an intuitive experience occurs instantaneously, you will want to slow the experience down to recognize and clarify the details in your mind.

Allow yourself to fully remember the intuitive experience. Then, signal the experience so that you have a personal resource state that you can recall at any time.

Bring yourself back to the present date, time, and location. Continue to breathe slowly and deeply, and enjoy the relaxation you feel.

When you're ready, open your eyes and congratulate yourself for the results you achieved in this exercise.

Take a few moments to write down the details of your positive intuitive experience.

Exercise 2: Now, use the following exercise to identify and clarify your internal signals for an intuitive experience that did not provide the results you expected.

Find a comfortable position for yourself. Close your eyes and take three slow and deep breaths.

Recall an unsuccessful intuitive experience, including the location, people, and any other related details. If you cannot recall one, make one up.

Continue to breathe slow and deep, and as you do begin to feel your entire body relaxing from your toes and running completely through your body to the top of your head.

Take a couple of moments to enjoy this relaxation and begin to recognize the complete details and characteristics of this unsuccessful intuitive experience. Also, clarify the sequence in which these characteristics occur. For example, if your intuition was a visualization, what was its characteristics and in what order did they occur? If it was a combination of visual, auditory, and/or feeling characteristics, what were they and in what order did they occur?

Now, take time to imagine the details of your unsuccessful intuitive experience. Because an intuitive experience occurs instantaneously, you will want to slow the experience down to recognize and clarify the details in your mind.

Allow yourself to fully remember this intuitive experience and distinguish how the characteristics of this experience differ from those of your positive intuitive experience.

Bring yourself back to the present date, time and location. Continue to breathe slowly and deeply, and enjoy the relaxation you feel.

When you're ready, open your eyes and congratulate yourself for the results you achieved in the exercise.

Take a few moments to write down the details of your unsuccessful intuitive experience.

In his book *Use Your Head: How to Develop the Other 80% of Your Brain*, Stuart B. Litvak said, "There are no recipes, no magic chants to awaken that 'sleeping genius' within you. You must do it yourself."[3] We emphasize that quote here to reinforce a word of caution about intuition. Intuition occurs because of information that lies within the subconscious, and therefore should not totally replace the importance of analyzing a situation and doing research. Allow intuition to be your guide in conjunction with the logical and rational part of your thinking strategies.

QUESTIONING TECHNIQUES FOR CLARIFICATION

Maintaining objectivity and clarifying the meaning behind our perceptions are important characteristics of great thinkers. Their natural curiosity and desire to develop a total understanding of some thing or situation enable them to use a series of questions to gather accurate information and expand their thinking. This results in the ability to quickly identify root causes of problems, formulate creative ideas, and establish innovative solutions. Using questions that gather the most accurate data is an important part of the clarification stage.

In terms of questioning, there are two skills that we emphasize to our clients. First, we strive for accurate information—that which is specific and gets as close to the actual meaning that is intended by the person giving the information. Second, we use follow-up questions. To illustrate this, we have created the formula: *Follow-up Questions Squared* or $(FUQ)^2$. The formula simply emphasizes the importance of going beyond asking one question. Instead, we ask a question to establish accuracy and specificity, and then ask at least two follow-up questions to clarify information received from the first question.

Since no two people understand the same words or sentences the same way, it is important to get as close as possible to a common understanding. This must be done by clarifying information in terms of what can be seen, heard, or felt, and then establishing a common relationship of terms.

Questioning is the most appropriate and effective method for moving to specific information and a common understanding. For example, when a person says something is "too expensive," it can have different meanings to other people. A response to help clarify the meaning would be to ask, "Compared to what?" Then, one can develop a common understanding from that comparison.

Here's another example. Perhaps we present an idea and someone tells us that it has been tried before and can't work. We will want to establish a common understanding between the characteristics of our idea and the one that the other person has in mind. It is likely that the two ideas are very different, but we will never know unless we ask for specific and accurate information.

The following list provides examples of unspecified information that will likely create misunderstandings if it is not questioned. Also included with each example are the questions that can be used to establish more accurate and specific information.

When a person_____	Then we should ask_____
Deletes information in a statement (for example, uses words such as, "too much," "too many," or "too expensive").	"Compared to what?" so that we can obtain more specific information and precise comparisons.
Does not specify nouns in a statement (for example, uses words such as "They said_____," "These ideas_____," or "That group_____").	"Who said?" or "What ideas?" or "Which group?" so that we can clarify the deleted information.
Does not specify verbs in a statement (for example, uses words such as "operating too fast," "controlling too much," or "working too hard.").	"How specifically is it operating too fast?" or "controlling too much?" or "working too hard?" so that we can clarify the unspecified verb.
Uses words such as "should," "could," "can't," or "must."	"Why should_____?" "How could_____?" "What would happen if you did_____?" "Why must_____?" so that we can determine the effect and cause.
Makes universal statements that include words such as "all," "every," or "never."	Respond with a question that uses the same word, such as "all," "every," or "never."

After we use an initial question to establish accuracy and specificity, we then apply the $(FUQ)^2$ formula and ask two additional follow-up questions. While the formula itself is easy, it does require practice in application. In the fast-paced environment in which we live, it is a natural tendency for many of us to ask a question and quickly accept the first response given—even when the response does not give us the full understanding of information for which we had asked. Therefore, we need to develop a habit for asking two follow-up questions to those important responses we encounter. To develop the habit, we encourage our clients to accomplish the following activity. Over a period of twenty-one days, whenever you ask an important question (and it's up to you to decide which questions are important), clarify the meaning of the response with two additional questions. Begin practicing with people you know well and have a good relationship—your spouse, children, friends, and trusted coworkers are all people with whom you can practice. It will also help you develop a questioning style that is genuinely sincere and nonthreatening. After several days, a comfort level for asking the follow-up questions will be established. Begin using the $(FUQ)^2$ formula with other people and in different settings, until the habit of using the formula is established.

A word of warning is in order when developing the habit of follow-up questioning. The style in which the follow-up questions are asked is important as the formula itself. Therefore, we highly recommend developing a style that exhibits a desire for topical interest and understanding rather than one of interrogation. We always want to make the other person feel comfortable and at ease with the questions we are asking.

Questioning Opinions and Paradigms

In some ways, great thinkers may be considered negative thinkers because they continue to say no to existing opinions and paradigms. When we go through life accepting the expertise of others without questioning or adding our own ideas and opinions, then we risk becoming lazy and stifled thinkers. For example, if we read a book or newspaper or hear or see a news broadcast on radio or TV, many of us will accept the information as truth simply because it has been written or stated in mediums that we have come to consider reliable. However, our thinking can be enhanced by questioning information that we are given. For example, we can ask questions such as, Where's the accuracy (or even the truth) in the information? What evidence has been presented to fully support the information and make it accurate and true? From what sources was the evidence gathered? How was the evidence gathered? Who is presenting the evidence? How is the evidence being presented? Are there any contradictions that make the information questionable?

Stereotypes and acceptance of other people's thoughts and ideas as true without checking the accuracy can significantly limit our ability to maximize our thinking strategies. The questioning of information may seem to be a negative approach to thinking. However, the questioning of information is an essential requirement for enhanced thinking and the development of the strategies for better thinking model.

Consider the following example of how negative thinking can develop in the clarification stage. One of the things that contributed to Edward Jenner's ability to isolate the cause of small pox was the way he formulated his questions. Instead of asking, "Why do people get smallpox?" Jenner asked, "Why do people *not* get smallpox?"[4] As a result, he evaluated the situation from a totally different perspective, thereby more fully clarifying the situation.

SUMMARY

The clarification stage develops objective understanding about what exists, and establishes our awareness and appreciation for continuous improvements. The thinking strategies emphasized within the clarification stage include perception, imagination, and intuition.

Perception thinking strategies encourage us to recognize perceptions as what they are—value judgments that need to be accurately interpreted by checking what really exists, presenting information in objective terms, and evaluating the value judgments based on what actually is at all times and in all contexts.

Our imagination thinking strategies give us the ability to form mental images, combine experiences for the creation of new ideas, and develop creative resources. We develop our imagination thinking strategies through visualization and personal resource states, both of which develop, expand, and improve ideas. Also, these thinking strategies enable us to recognize, modify, and apply our internal states in ways that make our thinking more productive in various contexts.

The thinking strategies of intuition are those that enable us to know something without conscious reasoning. While limited research has been accomplished about intuition, there are various techniques that we can use to develop an understanding about our own internal signals that let us know when to act and when not to take action in various contexts. When combined with reason and logic, the use of our intuition thinking strategies provides even greater levels of thinking and performance.

We found the following quote from *Optimum Brain Power: A Total Program for Increasing Your Intelligence* by Miriam Ehrenberg, and Otto Ehrenberg, to be a good summary for the clarification stage: "Brilliant thoughts and new ideas can occur to anyone who takes the trouble to turn old ideas upside down, inside out, and round about."[5]

NOTES

1. Max Gunther, *The Luck Factor* (New York: Macmillan, 1977), 125.

2. Anthony Robbins, *Unlimited Power* (New York: Ballentine Books, 1986), 72.

3. Stuart Litvak, *Use Your Head: How to Develop the Other 80% of Your Brain* (Englewood Cliffs, N.J. Prentice Hall, 1982), 100.

4. Miriam Ehrenberg and Otto Ehrenberg, *Optimum Brain Power: A Total Program for Increasing Your Intelligence* (New York: Dodd, Mead & Company, 1985), 144.

5. Ibid.

Chapter Six

Generation Stage

We've perceived, we've imagined, and we've even experienced positive results from intuition. Now, we have established the concept for a new product or invention, we have identified a problem we want solved, or we have clarified a process that we want improved. The next step is to apply creativity—to generate ideas that will result in a greater number of solutions, better process improvements, higher performance, or increased profits.

The generation stage consists of techniques for identifying ad applying the thinking strategies that will stimulate creativity. As a result, we increase our ability to generate ideas and solutions that achieve desired outcomes—while avoiding negative situations that can keep us from achieving success.

When it comes to people who exemplify the characteristics of the generation stage, two names come to mind. The first is Thomas Edison, and the other is Yoshiro NakaMats. The profiles of these two inventors provide us with an excellent awareness of the creative process and the thinking strategies that can contribute to the generation of ideas. Developing a basic understanding of the thinking strategies that Edison and NakaMats have used provides us with a base from which we can further clarify and develop our own unique thinking strategies for generating ideas.

During his life of eighty-four years, from 1847 to 1931, Thomas Edison had taken out 1,093 patents. This number represented the most patents granted to any individual until recent years. How could one person be so creative and inventive? What characteristics did Edison possess that made him one of the greatest inventors of all time? Answering these questions provides us with excellent insight into the thinking strategies that promote the successful application of the generation stage.

When we study the volumes of information available about Edison and his life, we begin to find words like initiative, perseverance, individualism, optimism, practicality, and motivation continuously used to describe his motos operandi and work style. The overall image of Edison's youth was self-reliance and enthusiasm. From an early age, Edison was a doer. Not only was he industrious and energetic, he was highly motivated and ambitious.

Science and reading were two activities that interested Edison. As a young boy, he would conduct numerous experiments in his bedroom, and had the capability to gather and process large amounts of information. Edison also had an enterprising nature and could always find creative ways to respond to needs and issues that arose in his life.

One of the most significant characteristics was Edison's practicality, and he would consistently apply the knowledge he developed in creative ways for practical applications. This practicality was a hallmark of his life, and an important objective for all of his inventions was their practicality to commercial use.

Edison had a strong desire to accomplish as much as possible in his life. He wanted to make the most of his life expectancy, so time was an extremely valuable commodity to him. For example, the story is told of Edison having read the three-volume work of Michael Faraday's *Experimental Researches in Electricity*. His reaction was, "I am now twenty-one. I may live to be fifty. Can I get as much done as he did? I have got so much to do and life is so short. I am going to hustle."

For Edison, inventiveness and creativity were useless if they were not combined with continuous optimism and confidence. His optimism enabled him to pursue many ideas, while his self-confidence was exhibited by a boastful personality combined with a showmanship nature. In many ways, his optimism and confidence kept him motivated in spite of the numerous setbacks he encountered during his life.

The pinnacle of his inventive and creative abilities occurred in his early thirties, during 1876 and 1881, at his laboratory at Menlo Park, New Jersey. This facility provided an environment that allowed Edison to apply what most of today's performance consultants consider creative thinking strategies. The laboratory was a very pleasant environment for Edison, and one that brought happiness and contentment to his work. He could allow himself to meditate or let his mind wander. He was free to focus on various studies of interest. Most important, he could accomplish what he considered to be enjoyable activities without constant and unwanted interruptions. While in the laboratory, Edison took on a leisurely pace in accomplishing his work, whether it was to spend time thinking about a current experiment or actively pursuing some new idea.

While he was referred to often as a "wizard," it is said that Edison did not believe in luck or wizardry. Rather, Edison always emphasized that it was hard work and taking time to "try everything" that enabled one to achieve desired objectives. In fact, his most famous quote, that "genius is 1 percent inspiration and 99 percent perspiration," emphasized his desire and belief for achieving the outcomes that were practical and useable.

While Edison's quote seems to indicate that he attributed his success primarily to hard work, his 1 percent inspiration was also a significant contribution to his inventive and creative mind-set. For example, he had a unique ability to conceive of things that no one else did, and his curiosity about the secrets of Nature enabled his mind to easily relate seemingly unrelated conditions around him. He had the power to concentrate on a desired outcome, while also maintaining an awareness of what his mind was conceiving so as not to miss some useful connection. He was able to recognize when something unexpected and unwanted would show itself. Then, rather than discard it as inappropriate, he would connect it in some way to one of the many projects on which he was working.

So, while Edison was extremely practical, and he preferred to be viewed that way, he also accepted and understood the importance that inspiration and connections played in the generation of ideas. Throughout his life, Edison maintained the motivation, enthusiasm, and methods that made him one of the world's most creative persons. His achievements were due in great part to what some attributed to the notion that "he invented the profession of inventing."

Another individual who exemplifies the generation stage is Yoshiro NakaMats. While his name may not be as widely known to most people as is Thomas Edison's, he is nonetheless highly creative. Dr. NakaMats holds more than 2,300 patents and has a staff of more than one hundred employees who assist him in his work. He has also been a consistent winner of the grand prize at the International Exposition of Inventors.

One of Dr. NakaMats's most widely used inventions is the floppy disk, the technology of which was licensed to IBM. He also invented the compact disc and player, and was the person who brought us the digital watch. He distinguishes between visible and invisible inventions, with the invisible inventions being those that are useful but not seen. A new way of teaching something or a new way to spark creativity in others are both examples of invisible inventions. He claims that invisible inventions are just as powerful and far-reaching as the visible ones.

In his book, *What a Great Idea!*, Charles "Chic" Thompson provides excerpts of an interview that he conducted with Dr. NakaMats.[1] The highlights of the interview provide some excellent insights into the characteristics that this creative and inventive person considers important. Interestingly, many similarities can be made between the characteristics of Edison and those which Dr. NakaMats uses in his work. Listed is our interpretation of the characteristics.

Balance.   This refers to the concept of initially focusing on practical instruction such as memorization, and then progressing to free-associating. According to Dr. NakaMats, it allows development of the best ideas. Balance also involves the ability to know when to focus on action and when to relax and allow things to simply fall into place on their own.

Highly Inquisitive.   Dr. NakaMats was described by the author as questioning versus telling and listening rather than spending a lot of time talking. This inquisitive nature involves a genuine interest in understanding, and it reduces the inclination to simply accept the status quo. It's a characteristic of sharing and interacting that promotes understanding, learning, and greater generation of ideas. To stimulate quick thinking, he asks the question, "What would you buy today if it were available?"

External versus Internal.   Dr. NakaMats was described by the author as being formal when needing to be formal and also comfortable with himself and others. The ability to avoid being consumed with his own thoughts helps establish a productive balance for being fully aware of what is going on around him.

Natural Curiosity.   This curiosity, combined with academic learning, was always encouraged and developed by Dr. NakaMats's parents. He states that "they gave me the freedom to create and invent—which I've been doing for as long as I can remember." This encouragement is crucial to creativity and the generation of ideas because it reduces the fear of failure.

Practicality.   Dr. NakaMats suggests to young inventors that the practicality of ideas rather than money should be a primary motivator. When it is, the emphasis is on the development of ideas that benefit mankind, and the result is that money will automatically follow.

According to Dr. NakaMats, a genius must be a well-rounded person, familiar with many things, including art, music, science, and sports and cannot be restricted to only one field of expertise. He claims that your best ideas come out only when you have perfect freedom. To encourage this freedom for himself, he uses a three-step process for sparking creativity. He emphasizes that in preparation for the three-step process, it is important that only the best foods be eaten and alcohol beverages are avoided.

Step One: "Static Room."   The first rule is you have to be *calm.* Using a "static room," Dr. NakaMats produces calmness through peace and quiet, with nothing in the room except natural things such as a rock garden and natural running water. He free associates in the static room.

Step Two: "Dynamic Room."   This room is dark, with black and white striped walls. Using special audio and video equipment, he listens to jazz, moves to "easy listening," and always ends with Beethoven's Fifth Symphony.

Step Three: "Swimming Pool."   In this final stage, Dr. NakaMats claims to have a special way of holding his breath while swimming under water, which gives him the best method of coming up with ideas. He refers to this step as "creative swimming."

Dr. NakaMats only sleeps a few hours each night, and then takes thirty-minute naps twice per day. He uses a special chair that he designed for his relaxation periods. He calls it the Cerebrex Chair. According to Dr. NakaMats, the use of the chair can improve memory, math skills, and creativity, and also lower blood pressure, improve eyesight, and cure other ailments. The chair sends special sound frequencies pulsating throughout the chair so that blood circulation is stimulated throughout the entire body, and synaptic activity is increased in the brain. He claims that one hour in his chair refreshes the brain as much as eight hours of sleep.

Unlike Edison, Dr. NakaMats claims that ideas are 1 percent perspiration and 99 percent "ikispiration." To achieve "ikispiration," he applies three elements of creation: suji—the theory of knowledge; pika—inspiration; and iki—practicality, feasibility, and marketability. Dr. NakaMats insists that creative success is the result of going through all three stages and making sure that your ideas stand up to all of them. The result is "ikispiration." He also emphasizes that today's computer technology saves time and eliminates the 99 percent perspiration that Edison incurred during his time.

GENERATION STAGE: INFORMATION PROCESSING, CONNECTIONS, AND MOTIVATION

Getting the most from the generation stage means developing the power of three thinking strategies: (1) information processing, which enables us to acquire and manage data in ways that promote the generation of numerous ideas; (2) connections, which involve the ability to relate seemingly unrelated conditions or information, resulting in the generation of many unique ideas; and (3) motivation—which involves thinking that causes, channels, and sustains our desire to generate the actions necessary to make our ideas a reality.

The generation stage also involves two important concepts that contribute to the application of our thinking strategies: (1) developing the ability to expand existing paradigms into greater opportunities—what we call paradigm expansion; and (2) learning and applying specific techniques that contribute to relaxation.

The concept of paradigms is important because most of us unfortunately go through life adapting to and fitting into mental boundaries that we have created for ourselves or that have been formed for us by others. Our ability to recognize those boundaries, understand the limits of those boundaries, and determine the actions that can be taken to expand those boundaries contributes to the achievement of improved thinking strategies and greater performance. Every experienced performance consultant knows that until people recognize their imposed limitations and accept the fact that they can move beyond real or perceived boundaries, it is difficult to achieve a level of thinking that is truly remarkable.

Relaxation is important to the generation stage because it allows our conscious mind to rest and makes us more aware of information that is available within our subconscious mind. Deep breathing, progressive relaxation, and optimal environmental sourcing are the relaxation techniques we have found useful in achieving desired results from the generation stage.

Information Processing

We live in an age where ideas, information, and technology increase dramatically with each passing day. Those of us who are willing and able to find a personal comfort level for accepting this tremendous influx of information, as well as dealing appropriately with a fast-paced and ever-changing environment, have a greater likelihood of generating ideas and achieving significant levels of performance and productivity. Therefore, the vast amount of information that exists today requires the application of practical techniques and thinking strategies that enable us to process and manage data efficiently.

It is very likely Edison would acknowledge that an enormous amount of information had to be managed throughout his life. He would probably also suggest that his research, experiments and discoveries were adding to the available volumes of information that were emerging during his life time. Edison, whether he realized it or not, was a productive inventor in part because of his information-processing capabilities. For example, when he felt the need to learn a particular subject, he would gather many books on the subject and spend hours reviewing their content. Another example comes from a period of time during the 1880s when Edison had more than forty inventions going on at one time. Every day, he would move from one invention or experiment to another, inspecting results and reviewing the progress of each. It is said that Edison was regularly collecting various pieces of information and storing them away in his memory.

Great thinkers like Edison and NakaMats have the capability to quickly analyze information and then make judgments about its relevance to current or even potential projects or situations. They have the ability to quickly find needed information and then instinctively know the important elements that are useful from the amount of information they have made available to themselves. Their ability to process large amounts of information is also related to their talent for storing and then recalling information as it is needed for some future use.

It's interesting to observe and assess our own informational processing strategies and capabilities. Like any other thinking strategy, information processing is uniquely personal in style and characteristic. Some clients are comfortable with the retrieval and processing of a small amount of information at any one time, while others can easily manage numerous sources and large amounts of information on a continuous basis. The latter group of clients prefer to confront a large amount of information and numerous activities going on around them all of the time. Edison, for example, had a tremendous amount of energy and was also in need of a very diverse informational environment. In contrast to those clients who prefer large amounts of information and numerous activities, there are individuals who prefer a more manageable flow of activities so they can be fully involved in one activity at one time. These clients are secure and comfortable with processing a lesser amount of information and a limited number of activities going on around them.

We can quickly determine our tendency toward information processing by observing the frequency at which we change the activities being accomplished and the amount of information we search out and apply. For example, do we prefer an environment that is consistently busy and demanding or one that is calm and reserved? The purpose for establishing our informational processing preference is to guide us in the determination of how we need to apply our style for greater performance. It's important to remember that either style is appropriate to the generation of needed ideas, with the primary difference being how information is processed to get the ideas. For example, those of us who thrive on large amounts of information and numerous activities will, at some point, encounter periods of distraction and overload. Those of us who prefer a lesser amount of information occurring at a more even flow will also have a level at which distraction and overload occurs. When an unacceptable level of distraction and overload occurs with either style, it is important to identify and implement techniques that reduce those characteristics that are interfering with productive information processing. When we adjust the level of demands that are causing unwanted distraction and overload, increased idea generation and performance improvement will result. Therefore, it is personal need and capabilities that should determine the level and amount of information that is necessary to generate ideas productively.

We distinguish between two forms of information processing techniques. The first relates to internal techniques which involve the acquisition, processing, and analysis of information. For example, quickly selecting an article from a magazine, acquiring essential points from the article, and analyzing the points for application to our work requires internal techniques. The second form relates to external techniques which involve the creation of an environment conducive to our preferred style of organization. For example, we can arrange our work area in ways that reduce distractions, if that is our preference, or that provide the sense of a busy and fast-paced environment, if that is what achieves desired results for us.

Internal Techniques.   These involve the techniques that allow us to mentally process such things as books, newspaper and magazine articles, reports, and other kinds of information quickly and efficiently. In our performance consulting work, the internal techniques involve a three-step process that includes purpose, preview, and relevance.

The purpose step helps us focus on what we want to acquire from the data we are processing. We focus on our purpose by asking three questions: Why do we think the information exists? What do we intend to learn from the information? What do we intend to do with any relevant information we acquire? Some possible responses to the first question might be that the information exists because it is relevant to a new and growing area of study, it summarizes actual results to plan, and/or it provides an explanation and justification for a new idea. Examples of responses to the second question would then be that we intend to learn specific details about the area of study, including reasons for its growth, we intend to learn if the plan was met, and/or we intend to learn about the new idea being presented. Finally, responses to the third question might be that we intend to use relevant information to determine the potential applications for the growing area of study, to determine what actions must be taken to maintain or improve results, and/or to determine the likely impact of the new idea.

The preview step helps us focus on quickly extracting the information that is most relevant to our particular needs. If we simply consider and apply the "80–20 rule," then on the average, 80 percent of some article, or report will not be applicable. So, we want to get to that 20 percent that is going to be the most essential information for us.

The preview step also helps us change our perception about the vast amount of information that is before us. That is, if we tend to be distracted by stacks of reports, publications, and documents, then we need to adjust the way we are perceiving those stacks. For many of us, it is less distracting to know that we really only have to deal with 20 percent of the total amount of information before us.

The first thing we do in the preview step is place time frames on the processing of information. For example, an article or report that is less than ten pages in length should be previewed in less than thirty seconds. Longer reports, those up to fifty pages, should be previewed in less than three minutes. The time required to preview will need to be adjusted according to the total pages of the article or report. Then, we accomplish the actual preview of material.

When previewing articles and reports, we check the titles, section headings, and look for any words printed in bold or italicized type. For relatively short articles and reports, we quickly read the first and last paragraphs of the entire document. For longer materials, we read the first and last paragraphs of each section in the document.

We have found that most clients are able to accomplish a book preview in less than ten minutes. A book preview is done in the same manner we use when considering a book for purchase. That is, we quickly scan the front and back covers, read the critical comments that have been included in the book, and then quickly peruse the book's forward, preface, and table of contents. As we do these things, we want to think about the appropriateness of the book's contents to whatever short- or long-term purposes we have for the information. Finally, we flip through the pages of the book looking for any unique words or phrases that grab our attention and we believe are important or relevant to the book's title, as well as being applicable to our ultimate purpose. Also, every twenty pages or so, we skim that page's content to acquire additional points or examples that are being provided. The preview step, then, enables us to quickly isolate that 20 percent of the information that is likely to be most appropriate to our objectives.

An important point to be emphasized related to the preview step is that it requires discipline, practice, and trust—discipline from the standpoint of applying the preview step for more efficient and meaningful information processing, practice from the standpoint of applying the preview step until it is done consistently and continuously, and trust from the standpoint of accepting that while we did not consciously preview 100 percent of the information, there is a significantly greater amount of the information available to us than we might realize. We have found that continuous use of the preview step achieves continuous success in the efficient processing of information and generation of ideas, and continuous success promotes continuous use of the preview step.

In the relevance step, we take a few moments to assess the information we have extracted during the preview step. Our assessment is not one of critique, but rather one of questioning to formulate a connection between the information we have previewed and its application to our short- or long-term objectives. Therefore, we apply a variety of questions that can help us establish informational relevance, but we do not limit ourselves to only certain ones. Rather, we begin with a few common questions and then let our minds take over to create more spontaneous ones. We have found this approach to be extremely enlightening. There are numerous questions that can be used and the following examples are only a start. What is the likely meaning of each key word or phrase that was selected? What could the relevance of the information be to our objectives? How does the information in the article, report, or book apply to our objectives? What information would have to be contained in the article, report, or book for it to be more relevant to our objectives?

External Techniques.   These involve the techniques that allow us to achieve a level of comfort for processing information within our environment. Information has no value if we are not aware of its existence or we cannot locate it quickly. One of the first steps related to external techniques is determining how information has to be "packaged" to enable us to achieve the greatest level of comfort and productivity. For example, if a computer gives us a level of comfort that achieves better information processing and generation of ideas, then we use a computer. On the other hand, if networking with people provides the appropriate comfort level to be productive, then we meet and talk with people to generate ideas. Some of the clients we work with find that both the computer and networking are excellent sources of information for idea generation, in which case we recommend getting on the computer and entering an appropriate chat room. The options and possibilities are endless.

Another important aspect of the external techniques is the arrangement of our environment so it is more conducive to our preferred style and strategies of informational processing. For example, we need to consider the arrangement of light, sound, colors, furniture, equipment, and objects, that provide stimulation or cause distraction. We want to enhance the arrangement of things that provide stimulation and reduce or eliminate those which distract us. When evaluating the arrangement of our environment, we consider three components: space, work, and time.

Space.   There are two things we want to consider about space. First, we want to eliminate distracting clutter, and second, we want to maximize the amount of space available to us.

Eliminate distracting clutter from work surfaces, shelves, and drawers. The key word here is "distracting." What is distracting clutter for some will not be distracting for others. So, we emphasize that the desired outcome here is to develop an environment that is stimulating to each of our particular styles, and one that enhances our ability to think and generate ideas. When we discover that clutter is causing distractions and reducing our performance, then it's time to take action, and that means eliminating the sources of distraction from our environment. Two specific actions that can be taken include (1) getting rid of the stacks of old newspapers and magazines; and (2) putting all papers (single sheets and reports) that are laying around into several stacks (and this is important—we *do not* start reading these papers as we put them into stacks because that wastes time and might cause us to want to save some of them). The first stack will be for any piece of paper or report that is not addressed directly to us—we dispose of this information immediately because it can be obtained from another source if needed. If we do need the information, or anyone wants us to have information from any of these pages, there will likely be copies available from the original source. The second stack will be for computer-generated reports that are more than seven days old—we dispose of these immediately because the same information is available from appropriate sources. It will usually current information within recent reports that are most useful. There is one more stack, and this one will consist of papers that *will not* be discarded. This stack will be for contractual documents such as purchase orders, invoices, or employment applications. Any piece of paper that can be considered a legal document will be placed in this stack. And when our environment is completely organized to our preferred style, this stack will be the one to get our urgent attention.

Maximizing space involves determining where we will put everything we need so that our home or work environment provides the stimulation that is appropriate to our informational processing styles and strategies. Some suggestions for maximizing space include the following:

1. Place essential tools within reach. For example, if we spend most of the day on the computer, then our telephone should be placed near the computer's monitor and next to an open writing surface so that both are easily accessible.

2. Keep only those things that are positive stimulators laying around or hanging on the walls.

3. Think vertically or horizontally, and use the space accordingly. For example, there are some of us who like information spread out vertically throughout our environment, while others prefer everything in one or several stacks. There are numerous things that can be done to use our space according to our preferences.

4. Use shelving where appropriate to hold books, reference materials, and other items that need to be readily available.

5. Determine the kinds of information that promote the generation of ideas and keep it close at hand. For example, if there are particular books that are motivational or inspirational, then we keep those handy. One of our clients uses a dictionary that he has had for years. He obtained it during the course of a very positive learning experience and has used it ever since. He claims that the dictionary not only helps him with the meaning of particular words, but the positive memories associated with it help him generate ideas when he picks it up and flips through the pages.

We have found that many of these examples can be applied to the use of computers as well. Examples include keeping computer files organized according to our particular preferences, having directories and files listed either vertically or horizontally on the screen, and using a screen saver that is appealing to us.

Work. What we do here is dependent primarily upon our personal preferences. The desired outcome is to structure our work so it contributes to our ability to keep information flowing smoothly and productively according to our preferred styles and strategies. Some examples that might help include the following:

1. Organize information into stacks, such as a stack of incoming information, a stack of outgoing information, and a stack of information that pertains to current projects or activities.

2. Preferably, handle every piece of information only once and act on it immediately. We realize this is sometimes easier said than done, so we suggest taking action on information using our "3-d" system—destroy it, delegate it, do it. Destroy it if you determine that the information will not be used. Delegate it to someone when you determine information is more appropriate to another person. Doing it means taking appropriate action on each item. When it is something that applies directly to a project or idea, we add it to our "to do" list and put the information in a project file.

Time. Many studies have shown that 80 percent of results are produced by time spent on 20 percent of activities. Therefore, information processing and idea generation can be made more efficient by using some kind of time management planner, system, or journal. These can vary from a three-ringed notebook with lined paper, to electronic organizers, to a planning program used in computers. The type of system is not what is important—it's finding something that we enjoy using.

Another important consideration is that the system be useful to our particular style and strategies. It is inappropriate to be forced to use a system that causes us aggravation and reduces our productivity. Whenever we work with clients who are trying to use (or adapt to) a time system that's not working for them, we suggest they get rid of it and find something else. A time system should provide three benefits: (1) keep us focused on pertinent information, ideas, and priorities; (2) help us remember dates and times for important activities; and (3) give us a quick source for important names, addresses and telephone, fax, and e-mail numbers.

We encourage clients to develop external techniques that are useful to their particular information processing style and thinking strategies. In other words, whether we are the kind of person who is comfortable with a small amount of information at any one time, or the kind who can easily manage numerous sources and large amounts of information on a continuous basis, the techniques we implement need to bring out the best of our style and strategies.

The continuous increase in levels and amounts of information currently available to us is not likely to diminish, but rather will continue to multiply at even faster rates of speed. Therefore, it is imperative to identify and apply information processing techniques that promote the productive use of thinking strategies within the Generation Stage. As performance consultants, our objective is to help people identify and learn their preferred ways to process information quickly, efficiently, and with the least amount of overload.

Connections

When we are able to relate some item—a condition, context, product, or piece of information—to another that seems to be totally unrelated, the result can be a significant increase in the generation of ideas. Making such connections is a very powerful thinking strategy, and one that, in our experience, is rarely taught or promoted for increasing performance and the generation of ideas.

A strong relationship exists between connections and the concept of serendipity. In the early 1950s, an American physiologist by the name of Dr. Walter B. Cannon presented a paper titled "The Role of Chance in Discovery" which discussed the role of serendipity in many important scientific discoveries. Serendipity has been defined as "finding valuable and agreeable things not originally sought for." Some may say that when serendipity happens there is an appearance to some that the courses of investigation and experimentation are indirect and poorly planned; yet the person who makes appropriate connections and finds the serendipity often discovers that missing piece of some puzzle, that scientific breakthrough, or comes up with that perfect idea.

Since connections and resulting serendipity are so powerful in the generation of ideas and other discoveries, it is important to identify and apply the thinking strategies that promote such a gift.

Information written about Thomas Edison's life occasionally emphasizes the connections and accidental discoveries that often occurred for the inventor. Also, there were numerous times during Edison's life when he was questioned about the role that "accident" played in his inventions. He would usually attempt to distinguish between accidental discoveries and his inventive work by saying, "Discovery is not invention, and I dislike to see the two words confounded. A discovery is more or less in the nature of an accident. A man walks along the road intending to catch a train. On the way his foot kicks against something and . . . he sees a gold bracelet imbedded in the dust. He has discovered that—certainly not invented it. He did not set out to find the bracelet, yet the value is just as great."[2]

This is not to say that Edison did not accept the idea of serendipity or the importance of making connections in his work. While he was quick to define the distinctions between discovery and systematic inventive research, it is clear from various writings that he appreciated and depended on both. For example, *Harper's Magazine* carried an article titled "Talks with Edison" in its February 1890 issue, in which he was quoted as saying, "Look, I start here with the intention of going there"—drawing an imaginary line—"in an experiment, say, to increase the speed of the Atlantic cable; but when I have arrived part way in my straight line, I meet with a phenomenon, and it leads me off in another direction—to something totally unexpected."[3] Also, Edison seemed to be in agreement with Pasteur's opinion that "chance favors the mind that is prepared." For example, it is rumored that Edison was thinking about some of his light bulb experiments one evening when he began slowly rolling a piece of compressed lampblack (fine soot used as a black pigment) between his fingers. Eventually he noticed that a thin thread of carbon had been formed and realized immediately that the element could likely be the perfect material for the bulb's filament. Whether the story is true or not, it does emphasize the fact that we can achieve successful connections in part by being aware of what is going on around us and then immediately applying that awareness to the informational database we carry in our brains. Some of us seem to have the capability to do this quickly and easily, while others of us have somewhat more difficulty making connections among items that are considered dissimilar.

What then contributes to connections being made, and how can we develop this thinking strategy to achieve more connections within the generation stage? We use the term "linking" to refer to that which contributes to our ability to make connections.

Linking relates to our ability to make new connections between the learnings and experiences we previously acquired. For example, a salesperson who moves from selling copiers to selling insurance is highly successful because he is able to quickly connect the selling skills he learned when selling copiers to a totally different product and market. While the insurance product and market are dissimilar to copiers, the salesperson competently connects his knowledge and capabilities about selling to his new responsibilities.

Linking will occur rapidly or slowly depending upon such conditions as the strength of our previous learnings or experiences, how often we access our previous learnings and experiences, and how deep certain learnings and experiences are in our unconscious minds. For example, after attending a training program, a person immediately connects what she had recently learned to several improvements that can be made in her job, while a coworker with the same type of job and having attended the same training program several months earlier never took the time to make similar connections. In the case of the second person, the opportunity for linking to occur was further reduced as the strength of the learnings declined over time. Our experience has shown that it's not that people are unable to make connections, but rather that some have not been encouraged to practice their development and use of the linking strategy. In relation to linking, practice does make perfect, and continuous practice does increase our ability to make connections and maximize our linking strategy.

When we work with clients to develop their linking strategy, we begin by using exercises that emphasize the importance of finding similarities among one or more items. For example, certain words do not seem to have an apparent connection with each other. However, when asked to think about the similarity between the words, most of us can come up with at least one thing. Try this for yourself. What connections can be developed for the following words?

flower   lamp   lemon

There are no absolutely right answers to the connections that can be developed, but here are a couple of typical responses. "All three items can be set on a table." "All three items could be yellow." This particular exercise relates to the linking strategy and is useful when helping clients practice making new connections among previously acquired learnings and experiences.

The following exercise is another we use when practicing the linking strategy. List the kinds of skills that could be used among the following jobs:

Mechanic   Surgeon   Consultant   Receptionist

Responses might include such things as "diagnose a problem so that the correct solution can be made" or "determine what people need so the proper service can be given."

We also recommend various activities that can help clients practice the linking strategy. One particular activity involves going to a library and reviewing the contents of at least five randomly selected magazines. While accomplishing the review, we look for topics and titles for which connections can be made to our own work or a particular project.

This activity works amazingly well when illustrated by the following example. The CEO of a major manufacturer of hand tools wants to improve the service his company provides to its dealers and distributors. The CEO and his staff want to achieve improved service through more creative and sustainable methods than those that have been tried before by his and other organizations. In fact, they want to establish and implement a process that goes beyond a temporary enhancement to one that positively changes organizational culture in ways that increase and sustain service and performance. They have been attempting to come up with some unique service ideas, but none have been right for what they want to accomplish.

The CEO is presented with the assignment of going to the local public library and selecting at least five magazines at random. He is provided with the assignment's instructions, which includethe following: (1) neither the type of magazine selected nor its articles are important to this activity; (2) none of the articles need to be read and the magazines do not need to be taken from the library; (3) the important factor is randomly selecting at least five magazines and thoroughly reviewing only the contents pages of each one; (4) the titles and descriptions of all articles listed on the contents pages should be reviewed, and those which are determined to have interesting connections to the topic or project (in this case, the topic of service) are listed on a separate sheet of paper, along with the specific reasons for the connection being made; (5) when others are involved in the project, then the notes are reviewed with those people in order to brainstorm further details and stimulate ideas for creatively connecting the titles of articles to the project.

Now, it's true that many CEOs will initially balk at accomplishing the assignment. After all, they are "busy and really don't have time for libraries." However, the return on the amount of time invested by the CEO to accomplish the assignment is tremendous, as evidenced by the results to this particular project. First, this particular CEO is not one to accomplish just the minimum stated requirement, so he randomly selects eight magazines from the library's shelves. The magazines are *World Press Review, Popular Science, The Saturday Evening Post, Chicagoland Gardening, Civilization—The Magazine of the Library of Congress, Change—The Magazine of Higher Learning, Technology Review,* and *Psychology Today.* He reviewed only the contents pages of each magazine and recorded his thoughts and ideas on a separate sheet of paper. The details of his connections and thoughts are described below.

World Press Review included seven feature articles, one of which was an extensive cover story, and additional articles within eight sections. The CEO selected a feature article titled, "In Search of Respectability," and stated that he selected it because of the appeal that the concept of respectability had to his idea of improved service. He thought that the idea of building respect throughout the company and the dealer–distributor network was an important characteristic for the service initiatives he wanted to achieve. The title also caused him to establish several questions pertaining to service and respectability including: How could respectability be developed, particularly in terms of service? What does respectability mean to the employees of the organization, the dealers, and the distributors? Who currently exemplifies respectability within the organization?

The contents page of *Popular Science* was the next to be reviewed. It contained twelve feature articles, as well as articles within five departments. The CEO identified one title that stimulated a couple of ideas for customer service. The title was "Finally! Recordable CDs," and a description of the article stated, "the CD itself is being reinvented as a made-to-order medium." The reason for selecting the article title was because the CEO wanted to totally reinvent service within his organization. Also, the idea of "made-to-order" reinforced the importance that the CEO placed in going directly to the dealers, distributors, and employees to determine specifically the kinds of service that should be established and implemented, and in what form or medium.

The Saturday Evening Post included twelve feature articles and seven departmental articles. Two titles were chosen by the CEO. The first title "Our Social Duty," caused the CEO to connect the idea of achieving respectability through a closer involvement with the community and finding ways of servicing society as a whole. The second title, "The Trouble Is," was chosen by the CEO because it caused him to come up with an idea for an activity that his executive staff and employees could complete. He thought it would be useful to complete the statement, "The trouble is . . ." so that ideas could be generated about what the company needs to improve in order to achieve a high level of service and respectability.

Chicagoland Gardening included three feature articles and fourteen departmental articles. The CEO selected two titles. The title "Getting It Right the First Time" caught the attention of the CEO because it emphasized the importance that he had placed on getting the service initiative implemented right the first time. He had heard from CEOs of other organizations that many of the initiatives such as quality and service are short-lived because mistakes are not avoided from the beginning. The title also caused him to connect the importance of discussing potential problems and mistakes with the executive staff, employees, dealers, and distributors. The second title he listed was "Putting Children in the Garden," along with a line from the article's description that read, "Children can bring great imagination to the garden." The connection the CEO made between a garden and his organization was that like a garden, the service initiative for his organization needed to be prepared, tended, and nourished to get best results. He also connected the importance of imagination and getting various levels and functions involved in planning, implementing, and sustaining the service initiative.

Civilization contained seven feature articles, four columns, and nine departmental articles. The CEO found one title, "Faith in the World," that he connected to service. The article's description caught his attention because it included, "A change in humankind's attitude toward the world." He connected the statement to what he had been hearing about the importance of attitude change toward internal and external customers, and he felt it was necessary to determine exactly what those attitudes needed to be in order to establish and sustain the proper service culture.

The table of contents for *Change—The Magazine of Higher Learning* stimulated the most connections for the CEO. There were eleven feature articles, as well as articles within six departments. The CEO focused on six titles from the feature articles. The first was "Clark Kerr's Perspective on Leadership Challenges," and the description included the phrase "challenges for today's and tomorrow's leaders." From this article, the CEO connected the need for leadership in making the service initiative work, and the challenges of that leadership had to be identified and managed. The second title, "Who's Who: Higher Education's Senior Leadership," along with the description that stated, "those who represent 'idea' leadership" caused the CEO to generate the idea for forming an 'idea' committee on service. The committee would be responsible for finding, developing, and reviewing service ideas throughout the organization. The third article was titled "The Young Leaders of the Academy," and was said to, "reflect on the major challenges they face as well as on their hopes for higher education over the next two decades." The connection made by the CEO was the importance of identifying the major challenges for achieving service respectability, including how the organization could make service work over several decades rather than just a couple of years. The fourth article, "Illusions of a Leadership Vacuum," had a description that read, "effective leadership today requires a new appreciation of what helps develop a visionary organization with a strong culture." The CEO connected the service initiative to the importance of developing a vision and culture so that service becomes respectable and is sustained over time. The fifth article title was "Mentoring and Peer Relationships: Two Young Leaders' Perspectives," and the CEO made a connection to the portion of the description that read, "relationship with peers and mentors played a major role in developing the current cadre of senior leaders." He thought about the idea of establishing a service mentoring program in which those organizational members who were considered leaders in service could become the mentors for others in order to sustain the service culture. The last article selected by the CEO was titled "Connective Leadership: What Business Needs to Learn From Academe." While he did not develop a specific idea from the title, he did like the concept of "connective leadership" and planned to contact several organizations of higher education to find out more about its potential use in the service initiative.

The next magazine was *Technology Review*, which included six feature articles, three columns, and eleven articles within departments. The CEO selected two titles from the feature articles. One title was "Field Work in the Tribal Office," which had a description that stated, "At Xerox's famed Palo Alto Research Center there's a new factor in innovation: teams of anthropologists." The CEO thought the concept of using anthropologists was interesting and wanted to find out more about it, especially in terms of team building and organizational improvements. Another article titled, "Companies That Listen to Their Inner Voices" had a description that stated, "how America's most successful corporations navigate turbulent economic conditions." The connection made by the CEO related to the need for methods that would help his organization continuously review and improve the service initiative so it can be navigated through the likely changes that would occur over time. Also, the magazine's contents included an article titled "Internet Movie" within the Prototype department. The CEO thought it would be useful to accomplish service communications and training through the use of the Internet. The CEO also highlighted a column article by Michael Dertouzos titled "The People's Computer," whose description reads, "Computer developers should strive for simplicity, ease of use, and machines that are 'people aware.'" The CEO considered this title to be a significant find because it caused him to connect the need for the service initiative to be simple, easy to use, and properly communicated to make people aware of the service culture.

The final magazine was *Psychology Today*. It contained seven feature articles, six articles under the heading of News and Trends, three column articles, and two departmental articles. The CEO selected two titles from the feature articles. The first was "The Art of Overcoming: The New Science of Resilience," which had a description that stated, "Surprising new discoveries from the exploding field of resilience reveal just what it takes to turn trauma into triumph." The CEO made the connection between the article's title and description to things he had been wondering about in terms of what his organization needed to do to respond to customers with a greater amount of flexibility. He liked the term resilience as one that could be applied to the service initiative. The second article was titled "Feelings Without Fear," and a portion of its description was "Surrender to who you really are. . . and be fully alive." The connection here was in terms of the development of the organization's service philosophy and culture to get back to basics and focus on what the organization does best.

Results obtained from this exercise are extremely powerful and worthwhile, especially since the generation of ideas is significantly increased. For example, within only a couple of hours, the CEO in our scenario had gone from frustration over not being able to identify the right approach for his service initiative to total amazement and excitement for having made connections by simply reviewing the contents of randomly selected magazines. The number of questions and ideas that were established by the CEO increased his performance and helped him develop a variety of unique approaches to accomplishing his service initiative.

Motivation

As a thinking strategy, motivation is extremely important for creativity and the generation of ideas, and since it involves a positive mind-set and self-image, it is a vital element within the generation stage. If we can motivate ourselves to work enthusiastically toward being creative and generating ideas, then our performance, and that of those with whom we work, can be increased dramatically.

Motivation occurs because we have an intense desire to achieve a particular outcome. That desire then creates the strength we need to minimize both real and perceived obstacles that stand in the way of our outcome. When our belief in an outcome is strong, it creates the enthusiastic desire that moves us toward the outcome and motivates us to succeed. It is our internal motivation that continuously drives us toward improving, performing, or creating at greater levels. It is always motivation that drives us to action, and yet some people confuse action with motivation. Action is the result of motivation, and true motivation comes from the inner qualities that make up our self-image and encourage us to take action.

The generation stage involves the creation of conditions for ourselves and others that will arouse and maintain an enthusiastic desire to be creative. To accomplish this, we need to understand the conditions that motivate us, as well as those techniques for dealing effectively and efficiently with our motivational thinking strategies.

Identifying and clarifying motivational thinking strategies is achieved to a great extent by recognizing our needs in any given situation and at any given time. Individuals who study human performance describe the concept of needs in various ways, and yet they all agree that certain basic needs are common to virtually any human being.

A natural instinct and desire for most people is to find ways to satisfy the needs that develop within them. Most of us who are in the business of improving performance are well versed in the methods for satisfying needs through appropriate motivational strategies. Unfortunately, as we know too well, there are many people who lose their natural instincts and desires for responding effectively to the needs they experience. Some consider it useless to react to their needs because of negative experiences they have previously encountered. Others fail to motivate themselves because of past results that were perceived as less than desirable. There are as many reasons for people not responding creatively to their needs and desires as there are thinking strategies for motivating them. Therefore, it is very important to recognize the fact that while our needs may seem similar to those of other people, the thinking strategies we use to satisfy them are highly unique.

One of the most widely recognized and accepted models for explaining the relationship of needs to motivation and performance is Maslow's hierarchy of needs model. This model illustrates a set of five categories of needs to which people respond: safety, security, social, esteem, and self-actualization. Applying Maslow's model to the idea of motivational thinking strategies enables us to determine the particular needs that must be satisfied to move us toward the generation of ideas. Another reason that Maslow's model has value to the generation stage is because it does not emphasize a fixed and rigid order of need for any one person. It emphasizes the uniqueness of individuals and the unique strategies that must occur to satisfy the various needs that people exhibit at different times throughout their lives.

Maslow's model also emphasizes that people will continuously strive to satisfy some need. Once a need is satisfied it no longer acts as a motivator because another need will immediately take its place. The fact that every person is constantly striving to satisfy some need emphasizes the importance of identifying the particular needs that must be satisfied within each individual at any particular time. Also, it's important to understand that lower level needs on the hierarchy must be satisfied before the higher level needs take on any significant importance for driving behavior. Yet, once a person is at the higher level there are many more options available to satisfy those needs than were at the lower level needs. In general, unless the lower level needs are relatively well satisfied, the others will not play a key role in creativity and influencing the generation of ideas. This can be a challenge for performance consultants because it requires us to continuously adjust our methods for identifying the need at which we, or others, are operating, so that we can apply the appropriate motivational thinking strategies.

Maslow's Hierarchy of Needs.   Highlights of each of the needs from Maslow's hierarchy model are provided below, along with examples of corresponding motivational thinking strategies that could possibly be applied. It's useful to point out, however, that when applying motivational thinking strategies in our performance consulting work, the focus is not on analyzing a particular need to determine its classification on the hierarchy, but rather on the recognition and understanding of the existence of basic needs and the application of proper motivational thinking strategies that can move our clients toward self-actualization. Self-actualization should be the desired outcome for ourselves and for others. Therefore, determining and applying the motivational strategies that help us achieve that outcome is of utmost importance.

Safety.   These particular needs are linked directly to sustaining human life and include such things as air, food, sleep, and shelter. Any critical threats to these needs produce tremendous desires for taking actions that will keep us safe. Safety needs are the strongest of the five needs on the model, and they are very strong motivators because they have to be satisfied for life to be sustained. Safety needs are also the easiest to satisfy, and most people, at least in developed countries, do not encounter drastic threats to their safety needs. However, it is useful from a performance consulting standpoint to consider how much of our behavior throughout the day is motivated by safety needs for food, rest, and relaxation, or some other basic safety need. Our performance consulting work has taught us well that people who are nourished, rested, and relaxed achieve greater levels of quality and productivity in their job.

An example of how ideas can be generated as a result of safety needs comes from the time in Thomas Edison's life when he worked nights as a telegraph operator in railway stations. While employed in that job, he also continued his experiments with electricity and modifications to telegraph equipment. As a result, he had the need to sleep through part of his shift as a telegraph operator. His solution was to create a type of timing mechanism that automatically sent out required signals that proved he was on the job. Edison's need for sleep enabled him to generate an idea and a product that helped him accomplish his desired outcome.

Security. The evolution of our species has developed behaviors within us that encourage our avoidance of any threat to our physical security. An emotional reaction of fear is the result to any threat to our safety and when adrenaline is produced creates the fight or flight syndrome as the response.

We experience more subtle forms of security threats than our primitive ancestors did. Situations that involve changes within our organization, changes to our job, changes within our family, and other similar situations are all likely threats to our security. When our security is threatened, it is primarily the response to an intangible perception that we have created in our mind based upon attitudes, past experiences, and established values. Therefore, a security threat is not the result of external situations but rather the way we internally define the changes and occurrences that take place around us. For example, two employees who lose their jobs at the same time will have different reactions depending upon how they define the situation in their mind. One employee's security needs may not be threatened because she sees the job loss as a fresh new start and opportunity for achieving her career objectives. The other employee considers the job loss as a total threat to his security because of the negative internal response he created for himself.

The response to security needs will be based on the self-image and attitudes that we have about ourselves. If our self-image and attitudes are positive, then perceived threats to security needs will be minimal. On the other hand, if we have negative self-image and attitudes, the response is very likely to be fear of the unknown. So, our need for security can motivate us to generate ideas for dealing successfully with change or other similar issues that threaten our peace of mind, our lifestyle, or our well-being.

Social. This is a very strong motivator, and relates to the need for acceptance by others. For example, acquiring a positive sense of belonging, teamwork, friendship, and love all contribute to the satisfaction of social needs. We strive to satisfy our social needs by doing things that cause us to perceive ourselves as socially acceptable. For some, social needs are satisfied by the type of position held within an organization, or the amount of money that is earned. For others, it is the size of home, the type of automobile, or the styles of clothes that are owned. Still, others might consider volunteer work as a positive response to their social needs.

For many of us, the threats to our social needs occur when we perceive ourselves as not being acceptable to the society in which we live. On the other hand, when we believe that our actions and behaviors are acceptable to the people around us and to society, we develop a stronger level of self-acceptance and confidence. Social needs are partially motivated by the external response we perceive having gotten from society, and to a greater extent motivated by the internal response that is based on our sense of self-image and the perception of our self-worth within society. Here again, Thomas Edison's life provides us with a good example for how social needs become a driving force for generating particular ideas that satisfy those needs. He had often described the criterion that guided his ideas, experiments, and ultimate inventions as commercial success or practicability to society. Edison was also quick to promote a new invention to society, thereby satisfying another aspect of his need for social acceptance. For example, when he finally perfected his "talking machine" (the phonograph) after working hours and days on end, he immediately rushed out to publically demonstrate it to newspaper reporters. It is reasonable then to assume that his inventions and his desire to quickly inform the public contributed to satisfying his social needs.

Esteem.   Sometimes referred to as ego needs, esteem needs are ones that contribute significantly to our self-respect. We all want to feel that we are worthwhile and that we can continuously make contributions that result in positive changes in our lives and the lives of others.

While social needs are satisfied by a combination of external and internal responses, our esteem needs will only be satisfied when we believe that our desired contributions have been satisfactorily achieved. Even if external responses to our contributions are positive, our esteem needs will not be satisfied until we accept those responses as valid. Therefore, in order for us to satisfy our esteem needs, we need to determine the responses that we must provide to ourselves. For example, when someone tells us that a particular idea of ours is excellent, yet we do not agree that it is, then it is important to establish exactly what we need to do—for ourselves—to reach the same opinion on the idea.

Self-Actualization.   Increased performance and continuous personal development are ongoing challenges for all of us, and our pursuit for self-actualization will be realized only when there is a match between our results and our value system. The needs of self-actualization only become apparent to us after all other hierarchical needs have achieved an acceptable level of satisfaction. This is because unsatisfied needs in the areas of safety, security, and social will consume much of our energy and keep us from focusing on those things that can satisfy the self-fulfillment needs. Therefore, until those stronger, lower level needs are satisfied, we will find it very difficult to maintain a focus that is powerful enough to achieve self-fulfillment.

Some of the most significant characteristics of the self-actualized person include acceptance of self and others, initiative, innovation, flexibility, and spontaneity. As Maslow states in his book, *Toward a Psychology of Being*, "The human being is so constructed that he presses toward a fuller and fuller being and this means pressing toward what most people would call good values, toward serenity, kindness, courage, love, unselfishness, and goodness." Therefore, self-actualization will drive the generation of ideas that promote and satisfy those characteristics. To simplify the application of Maslow's model to the generation stage, we have found it useful to separate the five categories of needs into two primary categories. The first category is self-preservation and includes the safety and security needs. The second category is self-improvement needs which include social, esteem, and self-actualization.

We use the techniques of signaling and reframing for responding to the two primary categories. You will recall that the signaling technique was described in the portion of Chapter 5 that dealt with the creation of a mental stimulus for imagination. Signaling is also a very useful technique for developing a more motivated state, so it would be beneficial to review that portion of the book again from the context of motivation. The following information describes reframing as a motivational technique.

Reframing.   In the spring of 1900, Thomas Edison determined that electrically driven vehicles could be more efficient compared to what he considered the "wasteful" gasoline engine. However, to achieve the desired efficiency, electric vehicles would need a storage battery that was quite different from the lead acid batteries of that time. Edison's response was to make such a battery. Unfortunately, it was a difficult and extremely time-consuming process, due primarily to the difficulties in developing an improved positive electrode. During the time that the battery was being developed, which lasted ten years and tens of thousands of experiments, Walter Mallory, one of Edison's closest friends, would visit him in his laboratory about once a month. Each time, he would ask Edison if any progress had been made with the storage battery experiments. After several months of not having heard any positive accomplishments, Mallory offered his sympathy for the lack of results that had been gotten. To his surprise though, Edison smiled and said emphatically, "Why, man, I've got lots of results. I know several thousand things that won't work!"[4] Edison's quote is a perfect example of reframing, and one that is used quite often by performance consultants and others.

Reframing is a technique used to put new meaning around a perceived set of "facts," and it can be a powerful tool for motivation. Since the hierarchy of needs model pertains in part to our reactions from both internal and external sources, reframing can be used to shift motivation in more positive directions. The desired outcome of all reframing then is to separate intention from behavior so that we motivate ourselves and others toward the satisfaction of hierarchical needs. For example, consider the numerous times that we as performance consultants have naturally used reframing to motivate clients in training and coaching situations.

The meaning we apply to an internal or external communication and our subsequent responses to the communication is context dependent. Therefore, when we change the actual *context*, the *meaning* of the context, or the *content* used to describe the context, we will change or reframe the original meaning.

Context reframing is accomplished by thinking of a different context that will cause us to respond differently to the same behavior. For example, consider the internal communication, "If I daydreamed less I would get more things done in my job." A likely reframe to that statement could be, "Some of the best ideas for doing a better job come from daydreams."

Meaning reframing is accomplished by thinking of a different meaning in a communication so that the new meaning causes us to respond differently to the behavior. For example, let's consider again the statement, "If I daydreamed less I would get more things done in my job." To reframe the meaning, we would want to ask ourselves something like, "What else could this behavior mean?" or internally think of an opposite frame or a different meaning. "What is it that I haven't noticed in this context that will bring about a different meaning and change to my response?" A statement like "Creative people always daydream" is an example of a meaning reframe.

Content reframing refers to actually changing the content of the experience. So, consider again the statement, "If I daydreamed less I would get more things done in my job." To reframe the content of this statement we could say something like, "Daydreaming can actually reduce job stress and help me get more done."

We use a two-part exercise in our work to help clients learn and practice reframing. Keep in mind that this same exercise can be used for ourselves when the need arises. First, we have our clients establish a statement that represents the description of an unsatisfied hierarchical need that currently exists for them. For example, consider the statement, "There's really no sense in me working harder because my job will probably be eliminated in a few months anyway." This statement reflects a need for security. Second, we ask the person to take a few minutes and really think about that statement from alternative points of view. We also ask the person to consider what his or her real intention is for the behavior or for wanting a particular need satisfied. Finally, after those few minutes have passed, we instruct the person to write down all of the opposite points of view that came to mind. At that point, we review the list with the person, ask for clarification of each viewpoint, and help the person select what they consider to be their most powerful reframe from their list.

Let's consider some possible reframes to the statement, "There's really no sense in me working harder because my job will probably be eliminated in a few months anyway." A context reframe might be, "Some people's best results are accomplished by working differently during times of drastic change." A meaning reframe might be, "Is it possible that your job could be saved if you decided to work harder?" A content reframe might be, "Hard workers are always in demand."

Our motivational thinking strategies drive us to be creative and generate ideas. When the right need is realized at the right time, a corresponding amount of motivation is developed within each of us. Motivational thinking strategies give us the power to generate high levels of creativity if we are willing to recognize the needs that are driving them. Learning from the characteristics of such people as Thomas Edison or Yoshiro NakaMats, and applying our own variations of their techniques gives us the ability to generate the actions necessary to make our ideas a reality.

Paradigm Expansion

When it comes to our creative thinking strategies, one of the most commonly used words today to describe our difficulty in moving beyond established ways of thinking is "paradigm." Thomas S. Kuhn wrote about the concept of paradigms in his book, *The Structure of Scientific Revolutions.*[5] In it, Kuhn describes the strong influence that rules, or paradigms, had on scientists' views of their particular work. He discovered that established paradigms acted as filters that caused scientists to either accept information and ideas that matched established rules, or reject, distort, or overlook incoming information and ideas that were not comparable to their existing structure of thinking.

The word paradigm essentially refers to the basic assumptions, rules, and even attitudes that have formed boundaries around our thinking about certain things. After many years of conditioning, these boundaries become increasingly rigid and many of us find it difficult to advance our thinking beyond them. And why should we? After all, for a very long time those boundaries have been a positive influence to our information processing and generation of ideas. They have provided structure and helped us analyze and respond to information quickly. They have given us comfort in recognizing what we already know while maintaining the status quo and reducing risks. Besides, there have been times when some of us have gone beyond established and approved boundaries during our lives only to be quickly pulled back; so it really can be safer to maintain, and work within, those established paradigms. Right?

Well, perhaps in some situations, dramatically pushing any accepted boundaries can accomplish more harm than good. However, never moving beyond any established boundaries will also keep us from making those advances that are so critical to our quality of life, or to the performance increases that our clients so desperately seek.

To emphasize this point, we ask our clients to list five significant advancements that have occurred over the last five to ten years. From that list, we then establish the boundaries that were exceeded with each advancement. We also ask them to consider where most people would be today if the particular paradigm or boundary was never exceeded. The result of this exercise is a genuine awareness of how movements beyond an established and acceptable paradigm will very often achieve positive improvements in the quality of life. For example, consider where we would be today if the following paradigms were never challenged: (1) a computer needs to fill an entire room and cost hundreds of thousands of dollars to be powerful enough to accomplish our business applications; (2) once a person's arteries become clogged, there is nothing that can be done to avoid serious or fatal heart attacks; and (3) employees have to work at a central office rather than at home in order for them to get their jobs done right.

Paradigm expansion, therefore, involves a concerted effort to stimulate changes that go beyond existing boundaries. This is certainly not the kind of challenge to be taken on by those of us who are "risk averse." Even for those of us who call ourselves performance consultants, the shear act of stimulating change during times when people are trying to reduce change, can be a tremendous challenge. Yet, some of us need to take the risks of expanding the paradigms in order to accomplish greater results. Then we need to become the coaches who help others learn to do the same on their own.

There are three simple yet extremely powerful actions we promote for achieving paradigm expansion. The first action is paradigm identification, the second is expansion of boundaries, and the third is expansion techniques.

Paradigm Identification.   We begin paradigm expansion by developing an understanding and acceptance for the role that paradigms play in our thinking. That is, our existing paradigms consist of established and familiar rules that we have come to accept over many years of conditioning—rules that have contributed to our beliefs in what is possible in certain contexts. Our rules and corresponding beliefs are really meant to help us by creating a guidance system in our lives. They act as a filtering mechanism that allows us to easily process information for a particular situation, select the most useable information for the situation, and quickly apply selected information to applications within specific contexts. Unfortunately, though, while this filtering mechanism helps us deal quickly with short-term results, it often gives us a false sense of complete accomplishment and keeps us from achieving long-term advancements. Therefore, we need to recognize and accept established paradigms for what they are—existing rules that enable us to find and apply short-term solutions within familiar contexts. Once paradigms are understood in this way, it becomes easier for us to identify the existing rules we use to filter our creativity which keeps us from moving beyond established boundaries.

When working with clients to accomplish the identification and awareness of paradigm rules and corresponding beliefs, we ask them to think about and create a list of the ones that have influenced them over the years. Initially, it is useful to establish the various contexts for the rules in which their paradigms are formed. For example, there will likely be different rules and beliefs within the context of family and other social paradigms versus those that pertain to business and organizational paradigms. There are also numerous rules and beliefs that can be examined within the contexts of existing products and services, as well as within certain industries and fields of study. So, we begin by focusing on the particular context within which the client's rules and beliefs exist. Once the context is established, the client can then establish a list of the rules and corresponding beliefs that exist within that context. The result is an awareness of rules that have kept us safely confined to perceived boundaries, thereby limiting our full creative potential.

The following steps can be used to accomplish the exercise for paradigm identification.

Step 1: Establish a particular context for their paradigms. For example, is the context an activity such as telephone sales, meeting planning, order entry, or some portion of manufacturing; is the context some product such as a computer, automobile, building, or machine; or is the context a process such as accounting, manufacturing, or management?

Step 2: Establish the known or perceived rules that pertain to the context. For example, a rule within the context of an order entry activity might be that an order entered after 3:00 p.m. cannot ship until the next business day.

Step 3: Establish the known or perceived belief that pertains to each rule. For example, the belief behind the order entry example listed above might be that all shipments are picked up by United Parcel Service by 4:00 P.M., and an order entered after 3:00 p.m. will not have enough time to be picked, packaged, and readied for pick-up by the shipper.

The chart on the next page illustrates examples of rules and beliefs within a variety of contexts.

Step 4: Review the belief and establish at least three reasons why it may be limiting or untrue. For example, one reason might be that UPS could schedule a later pick-up, another reason might be that UPS could schedule an early evening pick-up in addition to a late afternoon pick-up, and a third reason might be that new handling equipment enables orders to be picked, packaged, and readied in less than ten minutes.

Step 5: Determine the facts related to the reasons that were established in the previous step, and use the facts to modify or change the current belief. Changing the belief makes it possible to change the corresponding rule and expand the boundaries of the paradigm.

Expansion of Boundaries.   The next step in paradigm expansion is to determine the actions that must be taken to move us beyond the boundaries of established rules. Our self-imposed boundaries keep our thinking contained and give us a false sense of accomplishment by forcing us to be satisfied with only short-term solutions or quick fixes. Most of us fail to realize that these boundaries stifle

Rule	Belief
Pizza deliveries cannot be made in less than one half hour.	It takes more than that amount of time to make the pizza and get it delivered.
Training is only cost effective for very large organizations.	It's too expensive for small companies.
Television programs cannot be broadcast without commercials.	Sponsors are required to pay for the programming.
Computers need to be the size of rooms.	The larger the computer is the more power and memory it will have.
A person's level of intelligence cannot be increased after a certain age.	Intelligence is a function of a person's capacity for learning which decreases as he or she gets older.
A car's spare tire must be the same size as the other four tires.	Anything smaller will not support the weight of the automobile.
A newspaper page has to be approximately 13.5" wide by 22" high.	That's what people are used to, and besides, the newspaper printing presses are designed for that size.
Book stores should focus entirely on selling only books and magazines.	Selling beverages and snacks would keep customers loitering around the store.
Educational programs should be presented in a serious and nonhumorous manner.	People will only take education seriously when it is presented using methods that are highly structured and somber.
It is impossible to accurately predict the activity of a tornado.	Tornados are too unpredictable and therefore cannot be accurately tracked.
The market within our northeast territory is completely saturated with our products.	We have sold all potential customers and filled all existing applications.

our freedom and initiative to go beyond the limits we or others have set for us. Accepting the responsibility to change our established rules and expand the limits of our boundaries promotes the generation of more creative ideas, the establishment of long-term alternatives that achieve greater results, and the creation and implementation of new paradigms.

The expansion of boundaries requires an attitude and commitment for wanting to achieve continuous improvements that go beyond quick fixes. It also involves the desire to move beyond the status quo and fully accept the premise that anything is possible. Like any attitudinal change, it requires each and every person to find the spark that will be his or her own driving force for changing existing paradigms. As performance consultants, we can certainly help our clients find their particular spark, but in the end it's up to them to turn the spark into a flame. For example, we can help clients identify their motivational needs and point them in the right direction for satisfying those needs, and we can also help them understand the personal values and beliefs behind their existing rules and how new ones can be established, but the commitment that fans the flame to move them beyond existing thinking toward expanded boundaries is ultimately their responsibility.

Expansion Techniques.   The third step in paradigm expansion is to apply techniques that help stimulate our thinking beyond the currently accepted boundaries of knowledge and technology. It's one thing to have the desire to expand existing boundaries, and it's quite another to know how to go about expanding them. Therefore, knowing and applying the following expansion techniques can promote creative thinking and the generation of ideas for long-term improvements. We have used Post-it[®6] notes as the example for each of the following techniques in order to illustrate how one particular product can be applied within each technique.

Technique 1—Application: This refers to where and how something is used, and involves identifying new ways and places for its use. For example, Post-it® notes are used for writing down a brief note and sticking it to something. Another application for the same Post-it® notes would be in project management where each Post-it® note has a particular project task listed and these notes can be moved around on a master sheet to establish the order of tasks for the entire project.

Technique 2—Adaptation: This refers to modifying or adjusting something so that it might be suitable in other applications. For example, Post-it® notes have been adapted for use in meetings by enlarging them to the size of flip chart paper so they can be written on and posted to walls.

Technique 3—Modification: This involves partially changing the characteristics or form of something, such as modifying the color, motion, sound, odor, shape, meaning, or form. For example, Post-it® notes are available in various sizes, shapes, and colors.

Technique 4—Expansion: This refers to enlarging something in some way, such as expanding time, frequency, strength, thickness, or value. An example is expanding the paper strength of Post-it® notes so they can be used more than once for certain applications.

Technique 5—Simplification: This refers to making something easier, less complex, or perhaps smaller, lighter, or more streamlined. For example, putting Post-it® notes in a holder that makes it easy to take the next note from the tablet.

Technique 6—Substitution: This involves using something in place of another, such as substituting ingredients, materials, processes, and so on. For example, substituting one process for manufacturing Post-it® notes with a more efficient process.

Technique 7—Arrangement: This involves putting things such as components, layouts, or schedules in a particular order. For example, listing ideas generated from a brainstorming session on Post-it® notes, and then arranging the notes in order of the best ideas that came out of the session.

Technique 8—Direction: This refers to the point toward which something faces (forward, backward, up, or down), or the line along which it moves (straight or curved). For example, the manufacturing of Post-it® notes might be made more efficient by changing the direction of some portion of the line.

Technique 9—Combination: This refers to joining one or more things together, such as combining units, or purposes, or blending ingredients and materials. An example is combining motivational quotes with Post-it® notes.

We have found the expansion techniques to be useful additions to brainstorming sessions in which clients discuss each technique in conjunction with the brainstorming topic. As clients brainstorm the possibilities within each technique, they find that a greater number of ideas are generated.

Relaxation

When we ask clients to describe the characteristics they exhibit when having difficulty generating ideas, we typically get responses such as tense, firm, stiff, stuck, exhausted, mentally drained, frustrated, worried, and alarmed. We then ask them to establish the likely causes for such characteristics and hear reasons like, "I get frustrated because the more I push to come up with ideas the harder it is for me to get them," or "It's exhausting to work my mind so much and not come up with any ideas," or "Being in a hurry to generate ideas actually causes me to get stuck in a continuous thinking loop that goes nowhere."

After our clients have described their characteristics, and what they believe to be the causes of such characteristics, we ask them to briefly describe how they eventually manage the cause of the characteristics so that the generation of ideas comes easier. Some of the most popular responses tend to be, "I forget about it and take a nap," or "I go do something I really enjoy doing," or "I tell myself to take a deep breath, lighten up, and get a change of scenery." Each one of these statements emphasizes the important role that relaxation plays in stimulating thinking strategies within the generation stage. The application of relaxation techniques can provide significant benefits, including the ability to better manage distractions, achieve a greater level of focus, and allow the conscious mind to settle down so the subconscious mind can get into action.

There are three relaxation techniques we have found useful within the generation stage: deep breathing, tensing and relaxing, and optimum environmental sourcing. While we provide our clients with instructions for each one of these techniques, we encourage each person to practice every technique in different situations, apply variations of the techniques, and even develop a combination of several techniques. The result is relaxation techniques that are personally customized to achieve the greatest results for every person's individual needs and preferences. We have included instructions that you can use when guiding your clients through each of the relaxation techniques.

Deep Breathing. Ask your client to get into a comfortable position. Some clients find it easier to do this sitting in a chair and others find that laying down gives better results. Then, guide your client through the following steps:

Close your eyes. Let yourself be aware of your breathing. Notice whether you are breathing through your mouth or through your nose. Notice the pace of your breathing—for example, is it fast or slow, or is it even or varied. Notice which portion of your body moves when you are breathing—for example, is your stomach or chest moving in and out as you breath, are your shoulders moving up and down as you breath. Now, observe your body. In your mind, inspect all the muscle groups of your body and notice where you feel tension. Take about one minute to do this. Return to your breathing. Begin breathing in deeply through your nose. Then exhale slowly through your mouth. Breathe deeply and evenly. As you slowly exhale, allow those muscle groups that have tension to relax, and notice what they do. Notice how slowly exhaling allows you to relax the tense muscles. Go on breathing deeply and evenly for a minute and notice what you feel throughout your body. Continue breathing in and out—slowly . . . deeply . . . evenly. Now, inhale to the count of four, and *hold it.* Hold your breath for the count of *four.* And, exhale slowly to a count of *eight.* Breathe slowly and evenly. As you exhale slowly, notice what you feel throughout your body. Breathe in with a count of *four.* Hold to a count of *four.* And exhale to a count of *eight.* Go on breathing at this rate and continue to experience the relaxation that is occurring throughout your body. Continue to do this for several minutes. Then, begin to let your mind wander, allowing every thought to travel in and out of your consciousness. Become aware of the thoughts that develop and take a few minutes to calmly guide them in and out of your conscious mind. Tell yourself that each of these thoughts has a connection to the generation of ideas and solutions, and the most relevant thought will become apparent after this relaxation exercise.

Continue to let the client experience the relaxation for several minutes and then continue with the following directions:

Before opening your eyes, it is helpful to return to a wakened state by doing several movements. First, move your hands and arms about. Second, move your legs and feet about. Third, rotate your head. Fourth, open your eyes, and sit up straight. Notice how you feel. Now, take a few minutes to write down the relevant thoughts that came to you during this relaxation exercise.

Tensing and Relaxing. This exercise is accomplished by slightly tensing and then relaxing certain muscles of the body so that we can become aware of the differences between being tense and feeling relaxed. We emphasize to our clients that this particular exercise should be done slowly and gradually, or if they have any back, neck, or other muscle–skeletal problems with their bodies they may not want to do this exercise at all. For those clients who are agreeable to doing this exercise, you can guide them through the following steps:

Breathe normally throughout the exercise. Begin this exercise by slightly tensing a particular muscle, or group of muscles, for about five to ten seconds, and then slowly releasing the tension. For example, begin by gradually clenching your fist as tightly as you think is appropriate, and then slowly relax the tension by unclenching your fist. Next, for about thirty to forty-five seconds, remain still and concentrate on the relaxation that is felt after releasing the tension. Proceed to another muscle or group of muscles (such as shoulders, stomach, thighs, or toes) and repeat the tensing and relaxing of the muscle. Become aware of the differences between the tense muscle and the relaxed muscle.

We often accomplish this exercise with clients by taking them through the following portions of the body, reminding them to *not* do any portion that they think would cause severe pain or discomfort. Also, as clients accomplish each exercise, they need to pause and relax for about thirty to forty-five seconds after tensing any one of these portions of the body. The following body parts can be emphasized.

1. Hands: Clench each fist separately and feel the tension. Then, clench both fists together.
2. Lower Arms: Make a fist and bend each arm up at the elbow. First the right arm, and then the left arm.
3. Upper Arms: Stretch out your right arm in front of you as if you are reaching for something, and then relax it. Repeat with the left arm.
4. Facial Muscles: Tighten your face as if you are frowning or reacting to the glare of bright sun light.
5. Jaws: Clench your teeth.
6. Lips: Tighten your lips together.
7. Tongue: Push your tongue up against the roof of your mouth.
8. Eyelids: lightly close your eyelids. Then, close your eyelids normally and then raise your eyebrows while the lids are still closed.
9. Neck: Slowly and gradually bring your head back and then forward until your chin touches your chest. Hold your chin against your chest for only a few seconds and then release.
10. Shoulders: Move your shoulders up as if trying to touch your ear lobes.
11. Chest: Tense chest muscles by taking a deep breath and holding it in for four to five seconds.
12. Back: Arch your back.
13. Abdomen: Tense your stomach muscles.
14. Thighs: Tighten the muscles in your thighs and buttocks.
15. Lower Legs: Point toes toward your head then move them back to their natural position.
16. Toes: Curl your toes in toward the bottom of your feet.

After clients have completed any of these portions of the body, they need to become aware of the feeling of relaxation that develops and how the relaxation feels for them. Also, clients should become aware of the rate of their breathing.

Before opening their eyes, clients should take a couple of minutes to remain in the relaxed position. They can let their mind wander to think about things they will be doing over the next several hours and days where relaxation will be useful, and consider how their relaxation can help them improve their thinking. When clients feel ready to open their eyes, they need to count backwards from five to one, take a deep breath and say out loud, "I now feel relaxed and refreshed."

Optimum Environmental Sourcing.   This technique is accomplished for the purpose of determining when and where our thinking is likely to be at its optimal levels. Each one of us has certain times and locations that promote the generation of ideas more than others, so it's useful to fully understand and reinforce them. When asked when and where they get the best ideas, many people can identify at least one particular time and location. For example, some people say that their best ideas come to them while getting dressed in the morning. Still others say that just before they go to sleep is when ideas come to them. Knowing at least one time and location for ideas is good, but knowing several times and locations is even better. That's why optimum environmental sourcing is so important. It enables us to establish numerous times and places where the generation of ideas is increased.

Some examples of where our best thinking might take place are listed below. This should not be considered an exhaustive list and we encourage our clients to identify others to add to the list. Complete the following sentence: "I do my best thinking while_____."

Cooking	Playing
Flying	Walking
Bathing	Working
Gardening	Eating
Waiting	Meeting
Driving	Shopping
Reading	Talking
Shaving	Sleeping

After determining the optimum times and locations for generating ideas, we then determine the mental processing that occurs within us. For example, a client determines that he gets his best ideas while walking, either around his neighborhood or on the tread mill in his home. When asked about his mental processing, he indicates that when walking outside, he begins by focusing on the walking itself, including his breathing and body movements as he is walking. After several minutes, he starts looking around at various things while he is walking, and that starts his mind wandering and making connections to numerous other thoughts. As he allows his mind to wander, he begins to find answers to questions that he has had about certain things, formulate new questions that he wants to find answers for, and generate ideas for solving problems or managing his business. Interestingly, his process while walking on the tread mill is very similar except for the fact that he imagines himself walking around the neighborhood in an associated state, and also pictures in his mind the various images he might observe if he actually were walking outside. He is then able to get his mind to wander and make connections as if he were actually walking outside around the neighborhood.

SUMMARY

The generation stage consists of those thinking strategies that stimulate our creativity. Using the inventive genius of Thomas Edison and Yoshiro NakaMats as models, we find that the ability to process information, make connections between seemingly unrelated items, and maintain a high level of motivation all contribute to the generation of ideas. Also, the ability to expand existing paradigms and use techniques that contribute to relaxation further enhance the application of thinking strategies with the generation stage. Remember though that each of us has unique strengths and characteristics associated with each thinking strategy. Therefore, it is useful to identify and refine our strategies and those of others, so that the performance of our thinking continuously improves.

NOTES

1. Charles "Chic" Thompson, *What a Great Idea!* (New York: Harper Perennial, 1992).

2. Matthew Josephson, *Edison* (New York: McGraw Hill, 1959), 158.

3. G. P. Lathrop, "Talks With Edison" *Harper's Magazine* February 1890, 427.

4. Ray Stannard Baker, "Edison's Latest Marvel" *Windsor Magazine* November 1902.

5. Thomas S. Kuhn, *The Structure of Scientific Revolutions* (2d ed. Chicago: The University of Chicago Press, 1970).

6. Post-it is a registered trademark of 3M, St. Paul, Minnesota.

Chapter Seven

Prioritization Stage

It is a tremendously gratifying feeling to know we can apply our thinking strategies to clarify particular issues and then generate numerous ideas for solving problems, improving processes, increasing profits, and achieving any other desired outcomes. The realization that we can think creatively using our own methods and strategies, and the fact that the generation of ideas and solutions is entirely within our capability, is extremely satisfying. Each time we journey successfully through the clarification and generation stages, we should congratulate ourselves for the results we achieved and thoroughly enjoy that feeling of accomplishment. Then, we need to move onto the prioritization and activation stages of the strategies for better thinking model in order to make our ideas a reality. Doing so moves many of us to an even greater feeling of accomplishment.

The benefits from generating a large number of ideas and contributing to increased performance are realized only if our ideas are prioritized and then acted upon. Unfortunately, however, at the point of having generated a myriad of ideas, there are some people who either start taking action on the entire list of ideas and some who hold off taking any action at all. There are also those who fall somewhere in between that action–nonaction continuum, and those people tend to implement ideas with greater efficiency while also achieving greater levels of performance. Therefore, we have found it useful and productive to identify and apply the thinking strategies that enable us to find a point at which the most appropriate ideas are selected and action is then taken.

The prioritization stage involves specific methods that contribute to the selection and prioritization of ideas and outcomes before moving onto the activation stage. Action can certainly be taken without prioritizing; however, when this is done, the desired outcome is usually more difficult to achieve and can take much longer than anticipated. Prioritization helps us resolve two conflicts associated with taking action: the conflict of selection, and the conflict of target dates and deadlines. As a result, our ability to select the most meaningful ideas to act on is improved and our ultimate levels of performance are increased dramatically.

Our exploration of thinking strategies within the prioritization stage led us to a group of people who have the unique ability to be highly action-oriented and yet capable of directing their efforts according to clearly established priorities. The group is that of top sales performers, and the characteristic of their profile that relates to prioritization gives us powerful insight and examples into the thinking strategies they use. Specifically, we have determined that top sales performers use thinking strategies that analyze both the importance and the impact of their ideas and planned actions, and then apply either a quick or extended rate of response.

Our selection of top sales performers as a model for prioritization thinking strategies is certainly not meant to imply that other groups do not apply similar successful strategies. There are many top business executives, emergency room doctors and nurses, transportation managers and dispatchers, police and fire personnel, teachers, and others who exhibit excellent thinking related to prioritizing of ideas and situations. However, we needed to do our own prioritizing and select one particular group out of the many that are available for study. We determined that the prioritization thinking strategies of top sales performers were the ideal choice in helping us develop an awareness and understanding of our own unique thinking strategies for setting priorities prior to taking action.

PRIORITIZATION: IMPACT ANALYSIS

A common theme presented by top sales performers is that excellent results are accomplished by prioritizing required actions. From selecting target prospects to arranging calls with key customers—from establishing call objectives to formulating negotiation points—everything top sales performers do must be prioritized so that it is accomplished at the right time and in the right order. They understand the importance of being both efficient and effective—that is, being efficient and doing things right, and being effective and doing the right things.

The definition of prioritizing that we most commonly and frequently use is "to arrange activities in the order of their importance, and according to the ultimate impact they will have on desired results." That's exactly what has to occur for top sales performers, and the definition holds true for each one of us in any day-to-day situation as well. Priorities are established based on importance *and* impact. For example, consistently successful sales people have a thorough understanding for the importance of responsibilities, commitments, goals, and objectives. They think about priorities according to the impact their actions will have on those activities that are most important.

The importance and impact of priorities is also common in many other areas of our personal and professional lives. Consider, for example, the importance and impact of priorities within the healthcare field. A doctor would certainly not begin a surgical procedure until the patient is properly anesthetized. If a heart attack victim is brought into the emergency room at the same time as a person with a minor fracture, it is understood and expected that the heart attack will get priority over the fracture. Prioritizing by importance and impact is an essential ingredient for successful thinking in many situations.

There are those of us who have encountered difficulty or limited success with prioritizing. It's not that we don't want to prioritize, it's just that we have found the subsequent results less than we had desired. The reason for this dilemma is because many of us tend to prioritize our actions according to two elements: *deadlines*—or what things are due the soonest; and *people*—that is, individuals with the greatest levels of authority receive a higher priority over others. Unfortunately, these elements usually emphasize low-impact tasks over high-impact effectiveness. They also cause us to consider almost every item on our "to do" list as a high priority, and reduces our ability to achieve desired levels of performance.

Impact Analysis

The thinking strategy we have gleaned from our discussions and work with top sales performers, and the one we teach within the prioritization stage of the strategies for better thinking model, is what we call impact analysis. It is a strategy for thinking that helps our clients determine the risk and value of their actions (or the impact) in relation to the results they want to achieve.

There are two methods that promote and accomplish impact analysis. The first is what we refer to as *quick response* method and the second is *extended response* method. We tend to use both methods, but each one has a different level of importance according to our tasks, functions, and authorities. For example, in a company that manufactures a product, those individuals in departments such as research and development, marketing, and human resources will all have a greater use for the extended response method. Individuals in departments such as sales, production, customer service, and shipping will use the quick response method more often than they use extended response.

In service organizations, such as a hospital or restaurant, administrators and managers tend to use the extended response method most often because they are prioritizing activities that extend over a longer period of time. On the other hand, emergency room personnel in a hospital or the chefs and servers in a restaurant will use the quick response method so they can efficiently and effectively deal with activities and decisions that must be prioritized immediately.

It is important to keep in mind that every level and function within any organization will encounter situations that require the use of both quick response and extended response methods. However, the frequency of use is determined by which particular method of analysis is most conducive to the accomplishment of responsibilities and authorities in the most efficient and effective manner.

When helping clients learn and apply both methods of the impact analysis thinking strategy, we begin with extended response. It has been our experience that understanding this method first usually makes it easier for clients to then learn and apply the quick response method.

Extended Response Method.   This method involves six steps that together accomplish the prioritization of essential activities that occur over an extended period of time. The steps include: (1) think goals, (2) think priorities, (3) think activities, (4) think impact, (5) think importance and urgency, and (6) think focus.

Think Goals.   This first step is accomplished by having clients list the top three goals of their company (or any organization, group, or team) for a specific period of time, usually the current year. Top performers think about their goals in terms of "big picture" results and use a brief statement that represents what they ultimately want to accomplish. Goals such as "servicing customers," "providing quality products and services," "increasing market share," or "increasing profits" are examples of how they think about big picture results. We encourage clients to think about and list their top three goals in similar terms.

Think Priorities.   Top performers think about the priorities in conjunction with their big picture goals. Therefore, the second step is to have clients list the top three priorities of their department or team that relate to the company, organization, or group they chose in the first step. Then, clients compare their priorities to the goals of the company. Each client then needs to ask the question, "Do the priorities I have listed help accomplish the company's goals that I stated in the first step? If the answer is "yes," that client can move to step three. If the answer is "no," "I don't think so," or "I'm not sure," then that client needs to consider establishing more appropriate priorities.

Think Activities.   In step three, clients list the essential activities that need to be accomplished in order to contribute to achieving the goals and priorities listed in steps one and two. Top performers think of essential activities in terms of budgeting, improving performance and productivity, or maintaining equipment and other resources. Here again, the top performer is thinking in broad terms that relate to an extended period of time rather than focusing on day-to-day tasks like returning phone calls or attending the weekly staff meeting. Thinking in terms of essential activities versus tasks increases both efficiency and effectiveness in achieving desired outcomes over an extended period of time.

Think Impact.   The fourth step is of critical importance. Clients assign an "A," "B," or "C" rating (with "A" being the highest) to each one of their essential activities. Later, in step five, they assign a numerical rating to each of the letter ratings; however, the rating in this step is based upon what they think the impact will be for each item according to its risk and value. Top performers determine risk and value by developing answers to two questions. The first question is "What do I risk by not accomplishing the activity?" For example, there might be the risk of monetary loss, legal trouble, or poor quality and service, and clarification of the likely risk that may occur by not accomplishing the activity is important. The second question is "What value is gained by doing the activity?" For example, there might be the value of increased productivity, increased customer satisfaction, or increased profits as a result of accomplishing the activity.

After clients have answered the risk and value questions, they assign their letter rating. For example, an "A" rating would signify a high priority item that likely has a low risk and high value; a "B" rating signifies a medium priority item that likely has some risk but also has value; and a "C" rating is a low priority item that likely has both minimal risk and value. Establishing risk and value, even in a subjective manner such as this, contributes to the way top performers think about their impact on organizational performance and productivity.

Think Importance and Urgency.   In the fifth step, clients further establish the importance (high significance and value) and urgency (requiring immediate action) of the ratings they have assigned to various activities. In other words, based upon their numerical ratings, clients narrow their list by determining those specific activities that have (1) high significance and value, and (2) require immediate action. This is accomplished by giving a rating of "1," "2," or "3" to each of their As and Bs. Top performers typically do not rate the Cs further because they think of them as low priorities that should either be delegated or postponed.

Think Focus.   In this sixth and final step, clients apply four focusing questions to each one of their priorities. The four questions they ask are "Why do it at all?"; "Why me?"; "Why do it now?"; and "Why do it this way?" Our experience is that top performers use these four questions to improve their thinking about the focus that needs to be placed on the list of activities. The questions enable them to reduce their activity list down to those things that they absolutely must accomplish—now! The questions help them determine which activities should be eliminated (Why at all?), delegated (Why me?), relegated (Why now?), or refined (Why this way?).

Many top performers have a high level of competence in applying the steps of extended response method; so much so that the use of this method as part of their impact analysis thinking strategies comes quickly and naturally to them, resulting in highly efficient and effective prioritizing of long-range activities. Our desire then is to help clients develop similar capabilities and related thinking strategies. To accomplish that, we use an activity that includes a worksheet designed so that clients can think about, record, and apply information for each step of the analysis(see Figure 7.1). An important point to emphasize here is that filling out a form to accomplish an impact analysis is not the essential part of prioritizing. The activity is not meant to become a continuous paperwork exercise that reduces overall efficiency and effectiveness. Rather, the activity is meant to stimulate the use of the extended response method and each client's own thinking strategies on an ongoing basis. It is also meant to help clients practice prioritizing so that they eventually internalize all the steps and become proficient without the use of forms. Ultimately, the activity will promote the quick and easy application of the steps so that impact analysis thinking strategies are developed and used competently.

At this point, clients will have applied their impact analysis thinking strategies by completing the extended response method activity. It has been our experience that some clients will have quickly recognized the benefit of taking the time to prioritize their activities. On the other hand, some others will tend to think that in the time it took them to go through the six steps of this method they could have accomplished at least five things from their "in-basket." When clients question the value of the time spent prioritizing through this method, we encourage them to consider this question: "Had you gone ahead and accomplished those five things from your 'in-basket' without doing an impact analysis, would all of the activities have added significant value to the organization? Those clients who can objectively and honestly answer "yes," are ones who are already very good at quickly identifying the essential activities that need to be accomplished. However, a vast majority of clients will answer "no," and that answer reinforces the importance of taking the time to learn and apply the extended response method of impact analysis. Eventually, these same clients will discover that prioritization thinking strategies improve their ability to quickly establish their high value activities.

Quick Response Method.   Let's consider the quick response method of impact analysis. This method is used by top performers who are required by their functions and responsibilities to make quick decisions about the activities and actions that occur regularly in their jobs. For example, a retail sales clerk must quickly establish the priorities of activities within the department, particularly when several customers want to pay for merchandise, some others want to use the fitting rooms, and others want questions answered. An emergency room nurse or doctor must quickly diagnose the vital signs and conditions of patients in order to decide the priority of treatment for each. The dispatcher at a distribution center must quickly establish the priorities of shipments that are scheduled for the day and determine the best routes for drivers.

These and other top performers accomplish their jobs by quickly and accurately prioritizing the short-term yet essential activities that must occur. They do not fill out a form to determine the priorities because they inherently know which activities and actions must be accomplished. They also know which ones

Figure 7.1
Worksheet to Apply Extended Response Method

IMPACT ANALYSIS EXTENDED RESPONSE METHOD			
TOP THREE GOALS: (of company, organization, or group) 1) 2) 3)		**TOP THREE PRIORITIES:** (of department or group— that relate to the company, organization, or group goals that are listed in the left column) 1) 2) 3)	
ESSENTIAL ACTIVITIES (Must be accomplished to achieve goals and priorities)	**RISK / VALUE RATING** (Assign "A," "B," or "C" to each activity according to its risk and value)	**IMPORTANCE AND URGENCY** (Assign "1," "2," or "3" to each "A" and "B" activity)	**FOCUSING QUESTIONS** (Why at all? Why me? Why now? Why this way?)

they should respond to quickly and which ones need to be delegated or rel-egated. As a result, the establishment and completion of their priorities are fast and accurate. Impact analysis thinking strategies that apply to the quick response method include four steps: (1) think job objective, (2) think essential activities, (3) think proper sequence, and (4) think action.

Think Job Objective.   Top performers know and understand their most sig-nificant job objective. Everyone's job has one significant and overriding ob-jective, and each one of us needs to know what it is for our particular job. For example, the significant objective of the retail sales clerk is to provide customers with a satisfying shopping experience; the significant objective of the emergency room doctor is to diagnose and stabilize patients; and the sig-nificant objective of a dispatcher is to ship the right product to the right lo-cation at the right time. To accomplish this first step, each client must determine the most significant objective of his or her job.

Think Essential Activities.   Top performers know the essential activities that must be accomplished to consistently satisfy their job's significant objective. For example, a doctor knows the activities that must be accomplished to di-agnose and stabilize patients. While the activities may vary slightly depend-ing upon the condition of each patient, there are essential activities that occur for every patient. Therefore, in this second step, clients must think about and determine their essential activities, particularly in relation to the job's objective.

Think Proper Sequence.   Top performers have the ability to establish the proper sequence of the essential activities. For example, a dispatcher has to have trucks available for shipping products, but will not schedule the trucks to the warehouse until he knows that the product is in inventory and can be ready to load when the trucks arrive. To accomplish this third step, clients must think about and establish a sequence of activities that achieve the greatest performance and productivity.

Think Action.   Having satisfactorily completed the first three steps, top per-formers then decide the action to take *and* take it. They tend to make this step look easy because they know and understand the previous three steps so completely. The result is that taking action is second nature to them. For example, consider the retail sales clerk who has four people to be checked out, two people wanting to go into the fitting rooms, and one with a ques-tion about a current sales item. She can quickly analyze the entire situation, decide how to handle each person within the situation, and then take ap-propriate action; all the time giving each customer what he or she needed at that particular time.

We help clients practice and apply the four steps of the quick response method for impact analysis thinking strategies using a worksheet that con-siders their job's significant objective (see Figure 7.2). Even when a client's functions and responsibilities are related more directly to the extended response method, it is a worthwhile experience to also accomplish this activity. Here again, filling out a form to accomplish the quick response method is not the

Figure 7.2
Worksheet to Apply Quick Response Method

IMPACT ANALYSIS QUICK RESPONSE METHOD
The most significant objective of my job is:

Essential activities of the job are:	The sequence of activities is: (Rank the activities from the left column according to the sequence in which they must occur. Place a '1' by the activity that must be done first, a '2' by the next, and so on throughout the entire list.)

Actions I must be prepared to take in my job are:

essential part of the activity. Practicing and stimulating the use of the client's own prioritization thinking strategies is the desired outcome.

SUMMARY

The benefits from generating a large number of ideas and contributing to increased performance are realized only if our ideas are prioritized and then acted upon. Prioritizing can be defined as arranging activities in the order of their importance, and according to the ultimate impact they will have on desired results. Top sales performers and others understand the importance that prioritization has on their efficiency and effectiveness. Those same top performers are capable of applying prioritization thinking strategies quickly and competently.

The prioritization stage of the strategies for better thinking model involves the use of impact analysis thinking strategies. Impact analysis enables clients to determine the impact in relation to the results they want to achieve. There are two methods for accomplishing impact analysis. (1) The extended response method is used in jobs where activities are prioritized over an extended period of time. This method involves six steps, including think goals, think priorities, think activities, think impact, think importance and urgency, and think focus. (2) The quick response method is used in jobs where activities and decisions must be prioritized immediately and where actions must be taken quickly to achieve desired results. This method has four steps, including think job objective, think essential activities, think proper sequence, think action.

Chapter Eight

Activation Stage

Getting to the activation stage of our model means that for the most part we have clarified some need, generated creative ideas, and prioritized what we believe to be the best ideas to act upon. It is in the activation stage of the model where the greatest challenge lies, in that it will either make or break our success in terms of implementing an idea and achieving some desired outcome. It tends to be very easy for most people to identify, develop, and apply their thinking strategies within the clarification, generation, and prioritization stages. After all, the results that occur during each of these stages of the model are primarily intangible consequences of our thinking. That is, they are basically ideas, concepts, thoughts, impressions, opinions, dreams, visions, or intentions about things that could be achieved. They are not things that have been achieved, or are even likely to be achieved, and they will remain intangible results until someone takes action to make them reality. The primary reason is because even though each of the intangible results can be spoken, visualized, or written down on some priority list, they do not have the same level of risk as that which is associated with fully activating and implementing an idea, vision, or intention.

The full importance of the activation stage is illustrated by the following example. The U.S. Patent and Trademark Office issues tens of thousands of patents annually, indicating the abundance of ideas that exist. The number of patents issued each year is a strong and tangible example that there is a never-ending stream of ideas for new and improved products or services. These patents are the result of identified opportunities, and there is no shortage of opportunities when we recognize and accept their existence. It is interesting then to consider that the patents only represent a small number of opportunities for which ideas were generated and then patented. The corresponding consideration is to imagine the number of opportunities that have been realized but not acted on, and the vast number of opportunities that have yet to be realized. Having an idea for which no action is taken to make it a tangible reality is virtually the same as not having the idea at all.

In the previous three stages, our emphasis was on developing awareness and application for thinking strategies associated with the clarification, generation, and prioritization of ideas, as well as process improvements. Using the strategies for better thinking model, we can identify our particular thinking strategies and those of others. As a result, we can understand when thinking happens, how thinking happens, and exactly what happens when thinking occurs. We will continue to explore thinking strategies in that same manner within the activation stage; however, we have found it useful to identify the strategies that have contributed to action, as well as those that have restricted action. When implementing the activation stage, it is useful to consider the strategies we use to promote activation and those that tend to stifle our ability to take action.

There are at least five categories of thinking strategies that tend to stifle activation toward a desired outcome. We say "at least" because while we know there are numerous thinking strategies that people use to keep themselves from taking action, we have found that most of those strategies can be classified under one of the following five categories: lack of vision, lack of focus, lack of self-esteem, lack of planning, and lack of risk-taking.

In contrast to the five categories of thinking strategies that tend to stifle action, we also identify and apply five categories of thinking strategies that promote action. The five categories are based on thinking strategies found in entrepreneurs, rather than in one or two specific people. The thinking strategies of entrepreneurs tend to exemplify what many people would classify as action-oriented characteristics, and therefore provide us with a very useful profile that can be used to formulate the thinking strategies associated with taking action. These five entrepreneurial categories are vision, congruence, self-reliance, decisiveness, and risk-taking. They are not meant to fall within any specific order, and each one should be considered as interrelated with the others rather than viewed as independent categories that contribute to action; that is, the presence of any one of the categories within an individual will not necessarily promote desired action unless it is working in combination with the others. For example, while we may have tremendous vision, a lack of objectivity and decisiveness might be the thing that keeps us from taking necessary action. It is the identification and application of our unique thinking strategies within each category that work together to provide the impetus for taking action and achieving desired results.

A brief description for each of the five categories that tend to stifle action is provided below. Then, we have provided more detailed descriptions and exercises within each one of the five entrepreneurial categories that promote desired action. Information provided within each of the five categories will also contribute to a better understanding for how to overcome the issues associated with a lack of vision, focus, self-esteem, planning, and risk-taking.

CATEGORIES OF THINKING STRATEGIES THAT STIFLE ACTION

Lack of Vision

According to Webster, vision can be defined as "the ability to foresee something through mental acuteness." There is no shortage of stories about individuals or businesses that have failed to take appropriate action due to a lack of vision. The inability to visualize and describe some desired future result prevents the identification of issues and actions that must take place to achieve the desired outcome. Consider the individual who lacks the vision of clear career goals and gets caught up in a corporate downsizing. When he finds himself out of a job, his reaction is typically one of extreme concern about having lost his job, rather than formulating a positive vision about advancing his career.

Lack of Focus

We are using the word focus to refer to one's ability to concentrate and stay on a task so that a desired course of action is followed, and results are achieved. A lack of focus results in an inability to take necessary action. Our lack of focus can occur for any number of internal or external reasons, including boredom, procrastination, disinterest, distractions, and anything else that pulls us away from our course of action.

Lack of Self-Esteem

When we do not believe in ourselves or our capabilities, then we will not have the ability to formulate and take appropriate action. Over the years, we have encountered people who have described their ideas to us in great detail. Their descriptions clearly indicated how well they had thought through the ideas. Some told us how important they believed their ideas could be to solving some problems or achieving some needed improvements. Others told how their ideas for a new product or service had tremendous market potential because they responded to specific needs in the marketplace. But when asked why they hadn't moved ahead with their ideas, the response we hear most often is something like, "I don't think I could make it happen," or "That's much more than a person like me could handle."

Lack of Planning

There are those of us who seem to have it all together—a clear vision about our desired outcomes, an ability to focus our efforts toward the outcome, and a level of self-esteem that gives us the confidence needed to pursue our vision. In this particular situation, taking action isn't necessarily difficult, it's having a plan that ensures the success of the action we take. Jumping in and taking action that is not planned and calculated can limit desired results as much as not taking action at all. To some clients, this particular category will seem inconsistent with certain perceived characteristics of entrepreneurs, primarily those characteristics that emphasize how some people just "took a leap of faith," or "jumped right into" some action toward an outcome. We suggest that the perception that some people "jumped right in" and took action without planning is not really what occurred. While it may appear that no plan was made, our experience has been that those people, when questioned about the specifics of their action, had actually formulated some type of initial plan in their minds. Also, while these initial plans did not contain great detail or consider every possible contingency, they were enough to get the people moving toward a desired outcome. Then, as action toward the outcome progressed, they would quickly respond to problems or difficulties by adjusting their plan and taking revised actions. Rather than one master plan, they actually accomplished a series of smaller plans that developed along the way to their outcome.

Lack of Risk-Taking

The idea that people would intentionally want to expose themselves to the chance of injury, damage, or loss is foolish. However, what some of us consider extremely risky is simply a walk in the park for others. Many of us will view some people as having the ability to take high levels of risk, while we wonder why others fail to take the same level of risks we take. For example, some people enjoy sky diving or bungee jumping while others consider the risk of injury too great, or there are those who find the stock or commodities markets exciting and profitable while others refuse to risk the loss of any amount of money. Our experience tells us that the ways each person thinks about risk-taking will vary, and their level of comfort with risk-taking can be illustrated using a continuum where each person's level of risk is somewhere between low and high. Unfortunately, though, we will experience difficulty in taking action if all of our decisions are based on the same level of risk.

We refer to "appropriate" risk-taking to emphasize the point that a low level of risk may be the most appropriate thinking in some contexts, while a much greater level of risk may be the best action in other contexts. For example, risking ten thousand dollars of our total disposable income in a commodities trade for which we have limited or no data would be considered a high and inappropriate risk. On the other hand, if ten thousand dollars represents a small percentage of our total disposable income that we intend to apply toward a well-researched and calculated commodities trade, then the associated risk would be considered by many to be low and appropriate.

CATEGORIES OF THINKING STRATEGIES
THAT PROMOTE ACTION

Each of the categories mentioned earlier is described below, and we have included examples of how thinking strategies can be applied within each category.

Vision

Entrepreneurs have the capability to create and visualize future scenarios of their desired outcomes. These clear and vivid scenarios contribute to the entrepreneur's excitement and motivation for taking the action that is necessary to turn the vision into reality and achieve the outcome. Then, having mentally created the vision, the entrepreneur is able to create a vision statement that describes what the future outcome looks like, sounds like, feels like, and even smells and tastes like. For example, one of our clients had the desire to move to a new home, and while the desired outcome of buying a new home was strong, the corresponding vision was virtually nonexistent until we helped her create a visualization of the desired future outcome. As a result, the following vision statement was created.

My new home is within a ten-mile radius of my existing residence. It is a two-story building with dark red brick, and it's located on a relatively calm street. I mean, it doesn't have a lot of traffic going back and forth. I can see a well-kept lawn with a couple of small trees in front, and I can even smell some of the flowers I planted. My home is on the second floor of the building. When I enter, I can see that there is a large open area, like a loft apartment. I can hear mild echoing because of the size of the open area. As I enter the front door, I can see all the way across the room to where the kitchen is located. It has new appliances and has a very organized layout. I feel good about the openness and layout; it's a very relaxing environment. I can see myself sitting down at a counter that separates the kitchen area from the living room, and I hear my stereo playing in the background. I'm eating a salad and I can taste the French dressing.

Within a few months of having created this vision statement, our client had found and purchased her new home. She insists it looks, sounds, feels, smells and tastes just as it was in her visualization.

There are five specific thinking strategies that we have found many entrepreneurs and others use to create and enhance their visualizing capabilities. They include physical positioning, stimulating experiences, segmenting visions, controlling interference, and senses connecting. Each one is described below.

Physical Positioning.   Visualizations can become clearer and more vivid depending upon the position in which we place our bodies. For example, some people cannot create mental images while they are sitting upright or standing. Rather, they need to be lying down in order to create their visualization. Others find that they can be sitting upright but need to put their heads back so they are looking up. Some people prefer to stand rather than sit, some prefer to lie on their backs while others lie on their stomachs, and some look up with their eyes closed to get the best images while others like their eyes open. There are numerous positions that can contribute to our ability to visualize. The point we stress is that everyone has the capability of visualizing; it's just a matter of finding the physical positioning that enhances each person's experience.

Stimulating Experiences.   Sometimes our visualizations need a little help to get started, so we have found that certain thoughts or previous experiences can bring about a desired visualization. For example, the image of a favorite person, place, or thing is easy to visualize. Once that particular image is established in the mind, other images can be introduced into the visualization and then adjusted for color and clarity. Also, some clients find that certain sounds, feelings, smells, and tastes promote desired visualization. For example, some of us find that a favorite song causes remembered images to appear in our mind.

Segmenting Visions.   We have found that some people are overwhelmed by the thought of creating a visualization, and this distraction keeps them from creating a vision of their desired outcome. On the other hand, there are those who overcreate their visualization, which causes a large number of distracting images. Therefore, we suggest that the person who is overwhelmed begin by creating only one small segment of their vision and then gradually create additional parts to form a total image. The overcreative person usually finds it useful to select and slowly eliminate unwanted images from the whole visualization, until a more precise and manageable image is formed.

Controlling Interference.   This pertains to the ability to reduce or eliminate internal or external interferences that get in the way of vision creation. The interferences include anything that can be distracting and takes our minds off the task of visualizing. For example, we will encounter some clients who have a tremendous amount of negative self-talk as they attempt to create their vision. Internal distractions result from saying things such as, "I can't create pictures in my mind so there is no way I can form a vision," or "I'm not sure this vision thing is really useful," and will certainly keep people from creating a vision. Another interference example involves external distractions in the form of sounds and images. Some people simply increase their external awareness while creating an internal visualization and become distracted by the sounds and images going on around them.

Controlling interference requires creative responses because each person will have a certain limit at which the distractions end and the visualization begins. Our challenge is to find that limit for each person, and so patience is very necessary here. Some creative responses include (1) telling the individual to say aloud all of the reasons why he or she can't visualize and then when finished having the person create only a small segment of some image; (2) having the individual create an image to represent each one of their negative reasons; (3) having the individual close their eyes to eliminate distracting external images and then gradually develop segments of a desired visualization; and (4) telling the individual to close his or her eyes and create an image that represents the distracting external sound, and then expand that image to other images that gradually connect to the desired visualization.

Senses Connecting.   Many of us have senses that are stronger and more dominant than our sense of sight. As a result, our awareness of the internal images we create has a tendency to be much lower than that of our other senses such as hearing or feeling. Therefore, we can help and encourage clients to increase their visual awareness by connecting their dominant senses to visualization. For example, if a client's auditory sense is strong, we begin by having them recall a favorite song, poem, or quotation and then ask them to form an image that represents it. Typically, the result is that the client already has corresponding images to the song, poem, or quotation but was unaware of them until it was called to his or her attention. For those clients who insist they don't have a corresponding image, we ask them to describe in detail an image they would create as a representation. The same process is used if the person's dominant sense happens to be feeling, smell, or taste. For example, we ask the person to remember something that gave him or her a positive feeling and then create a visualization to represent that feeling.

When clients have developed a comfort level for creating visualizations, we help them accomplish the following exercise. It enables our clients to develop a level of competence for creating future visions of desired outcomes. We usually use a one-year time period for the exercise, and yet the same steps can be used for any time period. Here's how the exercise is presented to clients:

Step 1: Think of the time as one year from today, and think of yourself as being there in that time and having accomplished some desired outcome. Have the client tell you the specific date one year from the day you are conducting the exercise, and have the client describe the desired outcome that was achieved in present-tense language. Some examples might be "It's 7 June 2001, and I've started my own business," "It's 1 December 2002, and I became president of the company," or "It's 17 March 2003, and I have fully implemented the company's computer-based training process."

Step 2: Allow yourself to move fully into the future vision so that you are seeing your surroundings and other people through your mind's eye. Also, become aware of all the sights, sounds, feelings, and other senses that you encounter as you clarify the details of this future vision.

Step 3: As you formulate your vision for the particular time period, begin to write down all of the details that you are experiencing from the vision. Write the details in present-tense statements, and write down all information as it comes to you. An example could be, "I have fully implemented the company's computer-based training process on time and on budget. I am logging onto the system and calling up a list of training programs that are available through the company's Intranet. I am also reviewing a list of names of those who are scheduled to accomplish some of the programs. There are phone messages on my desk from people who want to talk to me about the current programs, as well as others who want to talk about getting special programs added to the system. My boss just came in and congratulated me on a job well done. He said he was beginning to see more opportunities for this new training process." It is not necessary to have the information in any particular order, and you should not judge or criticize your vision. Just get the details down in writing. These details established from your vision essentially become the outcomes that you plan to achieve.

Step 4: After getting the details of your vision down in writing, think about what you had done over the "previous year" to successfully achieve the results of your desired outcome; that is, from the time period for which you have established your vision, look back to the current day and describe all the things you had done to achieve the desired outcome. If you had visualized yourself on 17 March 2003, you will want to look back to 17 March 2002 and describe the actions that occurred over that time period. For example, some of the actions taken to achieve the implementation of the company's computer-based training process may have included establishing the need, benefits, and cost justifications for a computer-based system; determining the project's goals and objectives; obtaining project approval from the company's management; forming a project team to provide input and support and to accomplish various tasks; selecting and implementing the appropriate computer software and training programs; developing the training programs and installing them into the system; and/or testing the training process. There are certainly many more actions that could be listed. Here again, when listing the actions, their order is not as important as having a full list.

Step 5: Review your list of actions and prioritize the list according to which action would be done first, second, third, and so on. When completed, an action plan exists that can literally be used to move you to successfully accomplishing your visualized outcome.

Step 6: Take action.

Congruence

This refers to the harmony and sincerity we consistently bring to all aspects of a particular message, context, or desired outcome. Congruence gives us strength and personal power and can be recognized by the sincerity of our verbal and nonverbal behaviors. As an activation thinking strategy, congruence is one that can help us recognize our tendency toward taking or not taking action in a particular situation.

Incongruence, on the other hand, is mixed messages that create ambiguity for ourselves and others, and results in muddled actions and self-sabotage. Being incongruent about something usually means that we are having some conflict related to it, and that conflict expresses itself in inconsistent messages and an inability to take action.

Both congruence and incongruence will be either overt or very subtle. For example, consider the person who is asked how he or she is doing. The response the person gives is "I'm doing okay" in a very slow and monotone voice that seems to represent a depressed attitude. That kind of response could indicate incongruence. The person says "okay," but the mismatch between his or her words, voice tone and tempo, and perhaps even facial expressions gives an indication that the person is probably not "okay." In contrast, the person that responds with "I'm doing okay" in a quick and upbeat tone of voice representative of a positive attitude is very likely being congruent. He or she says "okay" and means it.

While entrepreneurs, like any one of us, will be both congruent and incongruent at certain times and about certain issues or situations, they tend to be able to quickly recognize this particular thinking strategy within themselves. Then, once recognized, they either maintain congruence toward a particular action or they determine the cause of the incongruence delaying action in order to resolve their conflict, so that appropriate action can later be taken.

The particular thinking strategy we use to be either congruent or incongruent can be recognized within ourselves by identifying the distinctions among our visual, auditory, feeling, smell, and taste senses. The characteristics of our senses when we are congruent and incongruent in various contexts give us valuable information that can be used to move us to action or at least make us feel comfortable about our reasons for not taking action. We use a two-part exercise to help clients determine the distinctions about their senses when they are congruent and incongruent. The following example describes our instructions to a client.

Part One.   Remember a time when you really wanted something, you knew it was right, and you were ready to take action. As you think back to that time and event, you can begin to see what you saw, hear what you heard, and feel what you felt, and you may also recall any particular smells or tastes at that time. These memories will help you recognize what it is like for you to be congruent.

Now, after you have fully remembered all of the important memories related to your congruent experience, describe the details of each of the senses you experienced. For example, if you saw certain images, describe what those images looked like. If you heard certain sounds or voices, describe what they sounded like. If you had particular feelings, describe the characteristics of those feelings and where they were located in your body. Become very familiar with all of the sensory signals that you experienced as congruence in your remembered situation. You now have a personal example of your congruent thinking strategy for that particular experience, and you can identify and use it again in the future.

An example of a response from Part One is

I see a one-story building that has a relatively modern design and about ten thousand square feet of space inside. I can also see people coming in and out of the building. These are very clear, moving images, and everything is in color. I hear the sounds of people talking and the sounds of traffic in the background. I remember telling myself, "This is it. This is exactly the building I need for my new business location." At that point, I feel what seems to be a rush of adrenaline to my stomach. Then, I feel myself stand upright, smile, and then say again, "This is it." I walk away knowing that I'm going to lease this building.

Part Two. Remember a time when you wanted to do something, yet you had concerns about whether it was the right thing to do, and you were unsure about the actions to take. As you think back to that time and event, you can begin to see what you saw, hear what you heard, and feel what you felt, and you may also recall any particular smells or tastes at that time. These memories will help you recognize what it is like for you to be incongruent.

Now, after you have fully remembered all of the important memories related to your incongruent experience, describe the details of each of the senses you experienced, such as the images, sounds or voices, feelings, and any other senses you recall. Become very familiar with all of the sensory signals that you experienced as incongruence in your remembered situation. You now have a personal example of your incongruent thinking strategy for that particular experience, and you can identify and use it again in the future.

An example of a response from Part Two is

I am at a job interview and I'm hearing a woman tell me about the position, and the qualifications needed for the job. There is very little that I can see because the images are black and white and not in focus. I can hear her tell me how great I would be in the position and she would like to offer me the job. I feel confused because I know I need a job, but there is a voice in my head that keeps saying, "Something isn't right." I hear the woman ask me what I think about the position and remember telling her that it's something I have to think about. I feel like I want to tell the woman I'm not interested, but I'm afraid that I might be wrong about what I'm feeling. Instead, I tell her that the job sounds real good but I want to take some time to consider the offer. I leave the interview having serious concerns about taking the job.

This two-part exercise gives us the opportunity to relive congruent and incongruent experiences. As a result, we can develop a clearer understanding for the distinctions between these two particular thinking strategies. Then, based on those distinctions, it is possible to recognize how our levels of congruency encourages or discourages our actions.

Self-Reliance

The action-oriented attitude of entrepreneurs is due in part to a reliance on their own judgment and abilities. This self-reliance thinking strategy is characterized by the entrepreneur's self-confidence, initiative, and decisiveness in various situations. The entrepreneur knows a good idea when one comes along and has the confidence to act on it and make it work. It is important, though, not to think that the entrepreneur's self-reliance means that he or she is not interested in the ideas and opinions of others. On the contrary, his or her self-reliance is grounded in a healthy self-respect and positive self-image that is exhibited by an appreciation for the contributions of others. The highly successful entrepreneur understands the value and importance of others' input and efforts, and uses self-reliance to appropriately evaluate the pros and cons of a situation presented by others. He or she does not allow unsubstantiated opinions of others to stifle action, but will delay action when the opinions of others make sense.

Another characteristic of the entrepreneur's self-reliance thinking strategy is the low need for recognition and approval. This characteristic is another strong contributor to their ability to take action because they are driven by the actual results of their actions rather than aspects of the action that result in recognition or approval. In other words, it is the anticipation and stimulation related to achieving a desired outcome that drives and satisfies the entrepreneur, rather than the action that is taken in anticipation of receiving some type of recognition or approval.

The extent to which we use our self-reliance thinking strategy in particular situations can be determined by recognizing three sources of information that have the greatest "authority" to us. That is, in a given situation we will rely on any one, or combination of, three sources of information: self, others, and data.

"Self" is where we rely on our own internal system of information and evaluation as the authority in a particular situation. We tend to be self-motivated in the situation, make our own decisions, and have a positive self-image related to the quality of our efforts and actions. For example, an individual may have a need to purchase a new car, and because she believes she has been successful purchasing cars in the past, she bases her decisions entirely on her own authority.

"Others" is where our decisions and actions are based on the responses and opinions of other people. We want to check with others before moving ahead with particular decisions or actions, and establish a level of comfort and reassurance from others about a situation. For example, consider another individual who has a need to purchase a new car. In his opinion, the successes he has had with similar purchases in the past were due to the input he obtained from other people, such as friends or relatives. Therefore, the action taken to purchase a new car is dependent on the authority of other people.

"Data" is where we rely on what has been written or documented relative to a particular action or decision we are pursuing. We want to review information contained in such things as research documents, texts, publications, and other sources of data. An example here would be a situation where a person wants to buy a new car, and to reassure himself that he is making the correct decision, he reviews the data contained in the car's brochure, automobile magazines, and technical bulletins.

Remember, too, that there are likely to be many situations in which we use a combination of self, other, and data in moving toward a decision and action. For example, a person has determined on her own that she needs a new computer. However, she recognizes that her technical understanding of various computer systems and software is relatively low. As a result, she talks with some people about her computer needs, as well as the likely equipment and software that could fill those needs. After gathering information from others, she proceeds to gather and review data about the systems and software that she is interested in purchasing. The computer magazines and technical reports that she reads give her enough information for selecting what she believes to be the appropriate system. This example illustrates the use of all three authority sources for one particular situation, starting with the use of the self authority to make the determination to buy a computer, then moving to the other authority, and finally to the data authority before moving ahead with an action.

Decisiveness

This refers to our ability to make a decision and take appropriate action when it is required by a particular situation. The decisiveness thinking strategy is one that gives entrepreneurs the talent for making quick yet appropriate decisions, or slow and calculated ones, or holding off from making any decisions at all. The strategy involves four steps: (1) establishing a need, (2) gathering relevant information, (3) evaluating the information, and (4) making the decision. All entrepreneurs and others tend to use each one of the four steps when making decisions; however, the variable that makes the strategy unique to each one of us is the time we spend on each step. For example, some of us will take a long time to establish a need and a very short time to make the decision. Still others will quickly determine a need and then spend a significant amount of time gathering and evaluating information before making a decision. Here again, neither example represents an inappropriate manner of decision making, as long as the end result produces the action necessary to achieve the desired outcome. Entrepreneurs have simply perfected the use of their decisiveness thinking strategy in various situations. The result is they instinctively know when and how to apply the proper amount of time to each step.

Here's an example to illustrate the application of this thinking strategy and some factors that can contribute to the amount of time needed by another person in making a decision. A marketing manager runs into the executive vice president's office and describes in detail how various dealers have called to let him know that the new product introduction is being very well received by retail outlets. The manager goes on to say that he did an informal survey of twenty-five retail outlets throughout the country and found the reaction to be very positive. He also checked production plans and current stock levels against incoming orders and found that production would need to be increased by 12 percent if they are to satisfy the demand. Without hesitation, the executive vice president gets on the phone, calls the production manager, and tells him to increase the planned production runs for the new product.

The executive vice president's decisiveness was quick and direct. As an outside observer, we could conclude that he spent a very small amount of time establishing the need, gathering information, and evaluating information. In fact, he also spent a minimal amount of time making the decision—he just made it. However, if we fully consider the details of the situation, we recognize that the executive vice president's decision was very appropriate. He did not need to establish the need because the market manager had established it through information from several dealers. He did not need to gather information because the market manager had already confirmed the need with several retail outlets throughout the country. He did not need to evaluate the information because the market manager had already established current production and stocking figures against the anticipated demand. The executive vice president simply needed to make the decision.

In contrast to the example described above, consider what the executive vice president's speed of decision making would have been if the market manager had only established the need without gathering and evaluating information that was related and necessary. Also, consider how quickly a decision would have been made if the executive vice president had a low level of trust in the market manager's capabilities. Reaction to these two scenarios would have given the appearance of slower decision making on the part of the executive vice president.

So, what may seem to be a quick decision at certain times or a slow decision at other times is actually the entrepreneur's ability to move effectively and efficiently through his or her decisiveness thinking strategy. As this is done, the entrepreneur determines if the established need and available information are sufficient for making a decision.

Risk-Taking

Many of us know that there is always a degree of uncertainty when taking some kind of action, and within uncertainty lies the risk. To a great extent, the entrepreneur's ability to be a risk-taker results from how he or she thinks about and reduces uncertainty. This is accomplished using a thinking strategy that includes four ingredients: (1) anticipate obstacles, (2) establish contingencies, (3) remain flexible, and (4) build confidence.

The ability to anticipate obstacles is accomplished by formulating a vision of some desired future outcome, and then determining the obstacles that might be encountered as actions are taken toward achieving the outcome. We help clients develop their ability to formulate a vision and anticipate obstacles by using a variation of the six-step exercise from the vision section of this chapter. The exercise we use for anticipating obstacles is described below.

Step 1: Get into a comfortable position and think of some desired future outcome. Then establish a time in the future when the desired outcome is to be accomplished, and provide a clear and concise description of the outcome, for example, "It's 15 November 2000, and I have doubled the revenues of my business."

Step 2: Associate yourself into the future vision so that you are seeing everything through your mind's eye, and "look back in time" to the date that you began to take action toward achieving the outcome. For example, as you imagine yourself being in the future date of 15 November 2000, look back to the date when you first took action on the outcome.

Step 3: As you imagine all the events that took place from the time you started taking action to the future date when the outcome was achieved, become aware of all obstacles that occurred during the entire time period. Write each of the obstacles on a sheet of paper or dictate them into a tape recorder. For example, the obstacles encountered while achieving the outcome of doubling revenues may have included (1) production problems, (2) shipment delays, (3) lack of qualified personnel, or (4) a downturn in the economy.

Step 4: Take time to look back on each obstacle you identified and describe the contingencies you had in place and how you successfully dealt with each obstacle. Write your responses on a sheet of paper or dictate into a tape recorder.

It is important to establish contingencies in order to have ready-made options available for responding to difficulties as we take action toward a desired outcome. As a result, the availability of such options improves the ways we think about risk. Our establishment of contingencies is actually a by-product from the visualization that was completed to anticipate obstacles. Our responses from Step 4 of the previous exercise provide us with the actions we took to establish the contingencies and overcome obstacles. It's simply a matter of incorporating those contingencies into our action plan.

Another ingredient for dealing with risk is to remain flexible. Flexibility enables us to adjust to the changes, difficulties, and obstacles that are encountered as we move toward the accomplishment of a desired outcome. A mind set of flexibility enables us to react positively to the likelihood of uncertainties and increases our capability for managing risk. Applying flexibility in our thinking actually opens our minds to greater choices, and when there are numerous choices there tends to be significantly less risk. This is because numerous choices will increase the level of certainty that exists for us as we take action. Actually, an important aspect of strategies for better thinking is the ability to be flexible so as to identify and apply various thinking strategies in many contexts.

There are many different activities we use to develop our flexibility and that of our clients, and some of them are described below. Here again, this is not an exhaustive list. We encourage our clients to be flexible with the activities we have provided, and to think about other activities that will develop their flexibility.

Activity 1: Drive to work, school, or shopping using several different routes.

Activity 2: Think of yourself as someone who takes more risks than you, and "be them" for several minutes to consider how they might think about risks.

Activity 3: Learn a new way to do something you have done the same way for a long time.

Activity 4: Change the thinking strategies you use in certain contexts.

Activity 5: Spend a day listening more than talking.

Activity 6: If you tend to be silent in meetings, offer more opinions.

Activity 7: Spend one week eating lunch at different times each day.

Activity 8: Switch where you usually sit (i.e., during meals or meetings).

Activity 9: Change the tone of your voice for one day.

Activity 10: Say "thank you" and "you're welcome."

The final ingredient for risk taking is to build confidence, and is illustrated by Figure 8.1.

We begin all of our thinking and all of our actions with certain amounts of fear and confidence in response to the perceptions we have about potential risks and the level of success we believe we are capable of achieving. The perceptions that contribute to our fear and confidence are unique to each one of us and establish our ability to continuously take new and greater risks. Our perceptions about risk-taking are unique because they have been established according to our past experiences, values, beliefs, self-esteem, what we think is possible for us in certain contexts, and the number of risks we have successfully taken over time. Our amounts and levels of fear and confidence change over time as we develop successes in various risk contexts.

We can get by in life by taking very few risks, developing a certain peace of mind in knowing that the particular thinking and actions we used yesterday can be used again today to achieve an "acceptable" level of performance and results. Many of us believe that since our thinking and actions have provided acceptable results without taking on greater risks, there is little incentive to move beyond the levels of fear and confidence that we have established

Figure 8.1
Building Confidence through Increased Risk-Tasking

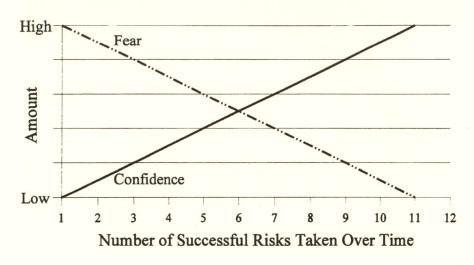

for ourselves. Yet, there are others of us who prefer to continuously take on a greater number of risks in order to advance to higher levels of performance.

Fear of unsatisfactory results or personal harm from risk-taking will cause us to maintain the status quo and result in inaction, while our confidence to take risks is developed as a result of new knowledge, understanding, positive beliefs, and even perceptions that we establish about our capabilities. Therefore, building confidence about risk-taking becomes a kind of catch 22 because we need to take more risks to increase confidence and reduce fear, yet we will not take more risks if we have a greater amount of fear than confidence about the risks we need to take. The way we think about failure and manage our fears will determine our abilities to either perpetuate or overcome this catch 22. The thinking strategy of most entrepreneurs in this particular ingredient of risk-taking is to calculate the risk, take the risk, promote the positive results achieved from the action, and learn from the negative results that were realized. The result is a continuously higher level of confidence to take on each new risk that is encountered.

While working with various clients, we have come to identify several characteristics that distinguish those people who continuously let fear reduce their risk-taking versus those who continuously build confidence for taking risks on a regular basis. The most common characteristics of fear thinking versus confidence thinking are listed:

Fear	Confidence
1. Thinks of failure as a final and permanent result.	1. Thinks of failure as a temporary situation that must be managed.
2. Thinks criticism is a personal indictment of capabilities.	2. Thinks criticism is a personal opinion and uses factual and objective information as a learning tool.
3. Thinks maintaining the status quo is a better course of action than trying something new.	3. Thinks that any results achieved from attempts at continuous improvement are worthwhile.
4. Thinks the avoidance of risk is a safer alternative to the potential failure that could result from a particular action.	4. Thinks that taking more and greater risk develops a cycle of continuous learning and builds confidence.

We emphasize that each one of us will experience some level of fear and confidence related to each risk-taking situation. We can encounter fear or confidence thinking, or any combination of the two, in any particular context or at any particular time. The type of thinking we apply is dependent upon our perception about the effect that failure will have on us in the situation in which we find ourselves. Also, when we perceive an incentive to change a current situation versus maintaining the status quo, there is a greater likelihood that we will have a greater amount of confidence to take the necessary risks. Individuals (like many entrepreneurs) who appear to be continuous risk-takers have simply discovered how to think positively about failure and objectively evaluate the incentives for either sustaining a situation or moving to a new one; that is, they do not avoid risk out of fear, but rather take or avoid risk as a result of a calculated decision.

When working with clients, we have found it useful to help them determine how they think about a particular context or situation so they can identify their strategies for taking risks and build confidence, if they so desire. When risks are avoided because of fear, clients need to apply thinking strategies that reduce the fear so they are able to make decisions in more calculated ways.

Fear associated with risk-taking is perpetuated when we continuously engage in various irrational thoughts. For example, the executive who has an idea for growing the business attempts to take action on the idea, but then worries that, "The board of directors will probably turn it down," "It's really not that good of an idea," or "Developing the idea could go over budget," all of which reinforces the fear of taking the risk. Fortunately, this fear can be overcome. The key is to interrupt and replace the negative internal images, dialogue, and feelings with positive thought patterns. To accomplish this, we use a four-step exercise that includes visualization, termination, replacement, and reward.

Step 1: Visualization.   Start by visualizing yourself experiencing some risk that you desire to take but are avoiding out of fear. Pay close attention to the sights, sounds, and feelings that are occurring in your mind. The result of this step is an identification of the specific emotions that occur for you when you fear taking risks in a particular situation. Then, when you recognize these emotions in the future, you can manage them more effectively.

Step 2: Termination.   After you have visualized and recognized your emotional state for avoiding risk out of fear, you can terminate the negative mental cycle you are in. The negative thought processes can be terminated by doing something physical like standing up, walking around, clapping your hands, or anything that successfully breaks your negative mental cycle.

Step 3: Replacement.   Immediately after you have terminated the negative thought process, you will want to replace it with a positive risk-taking experience. For example, you would think about an experience in which you took a risk, achieved a positive result, and increased your confidence. Recall how you felt before, during, and after the experience. Then, create a signal that you can recall when you encounter a future situation involving risk taking.

Step 4: Reward.   The final step is to give yourself a reward after taking a risk and increasing your confidence. The reward can be anything that reinforces your positive efforts for reducing fears associated with taking risks.

SUMMARY

Having a good idea and not taking action gives the same result as not having the idea at all, but having a bad idea and taking action is also the wrong choice to make. Therefore, it is useful to understand the thinking strategies that stifle action, as well as those that promote action. This understanding gives us the ability to recognize our reasons for taking action, delaying action, or not taking action at all. In some situations, our failure to act may be more appropriate than acting, while taking action in other situations may be the best choice to make. The point is that until we understand the thinking strategies that enable us to make the right choice, our use of the activation stage will achieve less than desirable results.

When we are ready to turn the intangible consequences of our thinking into a tangible reality, then we will be ready to identify and apply those thinking strategies that contribute to appropriate action. Our use of thinking strategies within the categories of vision, congruence, self-reliance, decisiveness, and risk-taking can provide meaningful results as we engage in the activation stage, for ourselves and for our clients.

Chapter Nine

Applying the Strategies for Better Thinking Model

Learning the strategies for better thinking model is really just the beginning of our journey to improved thinking and performance. Our development and application of the model is what enables us to continuously develop ourselves and others throughout the journey. Therefore, it is useful to consider the ways in which the stages of the model—clarification, generation, prioritization, and activation—can likely be applied in performance consulting situations. To accomplish this, we have developed this chapter using two scenarios from different applications and types of organizations.

The first scenario is based on a pure consulting project within a service business. It involves a consultant's use of the strategies for better thinking model in developing a group of executives' thinking strategies while also applying the model and their thinking to a desired outcome they had established for their organization. The scenario provides highlights of the process used by the consultant to apply all four stages of the model in order to achieve the client's desired results.

The second scenario describes a training intervention within a medical products manufacturer. Here, we have used the scenario to illustrate how a portion of the strategies for better thinking model can be applied by the consultant to achieve the client's objectives. The scenario specifically emphasizes the consultant's use and application of thinking strategies within the generation stage and highlights portions from the other stages of the model.

Both scenarios have been written from the perspective of the performance consultant and include details related to his or her application of the strategies for better thinking model within each situation. It is important to consider that the decisions and actions taken to achieve particular outcomes throughout each scenario are not the only ones that are necessarily appropriate. It is very likely that varying approaches by different consultants within each stage of the model will guide a client in slightly different directions, yet still achieve similar and equally positive results. The point is that while our unique styles, abilities, and thinking strategies provide varying approaches during a consulting project, the desired results will be very similar based on the established outcome that is meant to be achieved.

The two application scenarios we have provided are just the beginning to what is possible in the field of performance consulting and in understanding, developing, and applying thinking strategies within our personal and professional lives. These scenarios have been useful in helping us and others learn, practice, and apply the strategies for better thinking model in many other situations. Our hope is not to limit the applications for the strategies for better thinking model, but rather to expand its use in virtually every aspect of our lives.

SERVICE BUSINESS APPLICATION

This scenario involves a consulting project with a national freight services company (we'll call the company Freightco). The details of the project have been described according to several of the most significant discussions and actions that occurred between the consultant (Myron), the CEO of the client organization (Clarence), and various members of the client's executive team. Myron knows the executive team members well, and has accomplished numerous consulting projects for them in the past. His background in performance consulting and strategies for better thinking provides an excellent resource for the client.

Freightco is one of several major companies that provide freight rate services including processing, auditing, and paying freight bills. The company was formed in the early 1970s and was the target of several acquisition attempts during the early 1980s. It has been a privately held company since its formation and remains that way today. Freightco is headquartered in a major Midwestern city, and its management is highly experienced in the transportation industry. While Freightco's operations have remained relatively small in comparison to its largest competitor, it has continuously upgraded and improved its capabilities for providing efficient and cost-effective services. Freightco ranks second out of five major freight services companies in the industry, and is a close second to the industry leader. The executive team of Freightco wants to take over the number one ranking in the freight services industry.

The executive team anticipated the need and importance for taking a highly innovative approach to increasing the company's current level of business and becoming the leader in the industry. The CEO and executive staff have determined that significant business growth will not be achieved by the same thinking that built their business over the last couple of decades. Rather, they recognized that customers, employees, and suppliers throughout the industry are changing to such an extent that better thinking and innovation is required to achieve a leadership role within their industry. Therefore, the executive team decided to begin their quest for the leadership position by improving their capabilities for thinking and developing their intellectual capital. After identifying, developing, and implementing thinking strategies that contribute to their own intellectual capital, they plan to promote those capabilities and strategies for thinking with their employees, suppliers, and customers. The CEO and executive team have agreed to apply the stages of the strategies for better thinking model as a means of improving their thinking and achieving the desired outcome of becoming the industry leader. They have decided to work with Myron to establish the project's schedules and objectives and to have him coach them through the model.

Initial Project Meeting

Myron's initial project meeting with the executive team is conducted for the purpose of fully introducing the strategies for better thinking model and helping them "tune-up" for the development and application of the model's stages. He highlights each stage of the model by describing the concepts and thinking strategies included in the clarification, generation, prioritization, and activation stages.

Myron emphasized that strategies for better thinking was designed to help people recognize their capacity for exceptional thinking and to help maximize their natural thinking strategies. He also informs the executive staff that since each one of them uses uniquely personal thinking strategies, the strategies for better thinking model will help them learn, identify, apply, and improve those particular strategies. It will also help them identify each others' thinking strategies that can be applied to various situations in ways that achieve significant advances in performance.

Myron then introduced the "tune-up" portion of the initial meeting, saying that its purpose is to help the executive team develop a conscious awareness of their thinking strategies, and establish some of the issues they face when thinking. He emphasized the importance of taking time to fully accomplish the "tune-up," and the importance of slowly and patiently eliciting the details pertaining to their thinking. Also, Myron told the team that developing meaningful responses to the "tune-up" questions, exercises, and activities requires time, support, and encouragement.

Myron began the "tune-up" discussions by establishing the executive team's expectations, and helping them develop an awareness about the ways they do and do not think. Results of these discussions were useful in establishing the team's initial awareness for how they individually think and what each of them considers thinking to be based on previous experiences. The discussions also helped the executive team begin to formulate details of their desired outcome. Overall, the executive team's responses confirmed what Myron had discussed with Clarence when they began talking about accomplishing the project; that is, in order to become the industry leader, they needed to become more innovative, understand and improve their capabilities for thinking, and realize the full benefit of their combined intellectual capital.

The next step in the "tune-up" involved Myron leading Clarence and the other members of the executive team through several activities that helped them become aware of and appreciate the various thinking experiences and styles they could contribute to the team. In the first activity, Myron began by coaching the team through a series of questions designed to establish distinctions for when their thinking experiences were less than desirable and when they experienced thinking at peak levels of performance. Then, Myron helped the team formulate and discuss the systematic series of actions that resulted in the negative and positive experiences. This was useful for the executives because it established each of their primary characteristics, and the distinguishing traits or qualities of their thinking processes. Finally, Myron helped the team determine the answers to such questions as: "What causes you to come up with a good idea?" "What do you consider being the characteristics of the ideal thinking process?" "Where would the best thinking take place?" "What would the environment be like?"

Myron and the executives moved on to accomplishing two parts of the second activity. In the first part, Myron had each member of the executive team identify the thinking strategies he or she used when developing solutions to a problem situation. He had them begin by determining exactly how it is a problem and how it is not a problem. Then, he instructed each member to think about the problem as though it was entirely his or hers, and then as though it was someone else's problem. The result was an understanding for how thinking strategies vary among those contexts. In the second part, Myron helped each executive identify an idea he or she had wanted to develop but didn't for one reason or another. Myron coached the executive team to think about and formulate their reasons for *not* developing and implementing the idea. After those details were developed, he helped them formulate their thinking about an idea that they came up with and also implemented. Myron then helped the team develop distinctions between the two situations. The results enabled them to determine exactly how their thinking processes differed between the idea that was not implemented and the one that was implemented.

After the executive team members had established details about their thinking processes for each idea, Myron helped them discuss and develop responses to a series of questions that focused on the timing and location of their ideas; the process for coming up with the ideas; and the differences between their thinking processes for various ideas and in different contexts.

Myron then introduced the third activity, which was to help each member of the executive team clarify the characteristics and strategies of his or her thinking process. The discussion that Myron facilitated helped the members describe the significant parts of their thinking processes and the unique characteristics of each part. This activity also helped develop each executive's awareness for the mental processing that occurs when thinking about a problem versus developing and implementing an idea. They began to realize the characteristics of their thinking, including the pictures or other visual images that develop, the internal sounds or self-talk that occur, and the particular feelings that may have developed for each of them. Beyond that, Myron also helped them clarify the distinguishing traits and qualities of each characteristic.

Myron concluded the initial project meeting and "tune-up" by summarizing the results and instructing the executive staff to take time over the next several days to continue developing their responses to the questions and activities that were discussed. They agreed to meet again within two weeks to learn and identify their thinking strategies within the clarification stage, and apply those thinking strategies to the company's desired outcome of becoming the leader within their industry.

Applying the Clarification Stage

Myron returned to Freightco and met with Clarence and the executive team. Myron began by reviewing the results that occurred during the "tune-up" session and the thinking experiences that each executive team member had over the previous two weeks. After responding to questions and facilitating several discussions pertaining to particular results that had developed since the "tune-up," Myron introduced the clarification stage of the strategies for better thinking model.

Myron emphasized the importance of making continuous improvements for one's self and the entire organization. He stressed the fact that the primary purpose for the clarification stage is to identify and determine continuous improvement efforts. Myron also congratulated the executive team for having established the desired outcome of becoming the industry leader. Establishing the outcome illustrated their desire for the continuous improvement and success of their organization. However, such an improvement and achievement of the outcome required the ability to identify and apply thinking strategies. He described the clarification stage, including the thinking strategies of perception, imagination, and intuition that are included within the stage.

Myron asked the executive team to answer the question, "What do you perceive as being the characteristics of a leader within your industry?" He allowed the executive team to take some time to develop their responses to the question, which included such things as high quality services; value of services to customers; fast response to customer needs and requirements; competitive pricing; flexibility in providing services; highly capable employees;

continuously improving services to meet needs and demands; projecting a positive company image; and delivering what is promised.

In response to the list, Myron asked, "How do you know those things?" He waited as the executives looked around at each other and contemplated an answer. Clarence then said, "These are some of the things I hear from our customers." Another executive said, "I see our competition providing some of those things." Still another said, "Our sales people tell me about complaints that customers have about our service and that of our competition." Having developed the list and determined some examples of how they know about the leadership characteristics, Myron told the executive team that the first step in clarifying perceptions is to recognize that none of the characteristics listed are neither accurate nor inaccurate. The meaning behind their perceptions about what is occurring will assist them in clarifying and understanding the most important issues for becoming an industry leader. Those particular characteristics need to be interpreted and understood before actions are taken. Myron pointed out that great thinkers check out their perceptions and great business people need to do the same.

The executive team was then provided with a brief presentation in which Myron described what great thinkers do and do not do to accurately perceive experiences. He also coached them through several exercises to develop their understanding for how perceptions are established and the responses that need to be applied to determine an accurate meaning for the perceptions. Myron stressed that the reason for applying accuracy is so that value judgments are avoided and objective clarification is accomplished. Myron also emphasized the importance for determining what actually is versus what might be, particularly in terms of their outcome of becoming the industry leader.

Myron completed the introduction of the perception thinking strategy and asked the executive team to consider the following question: "Based upon the industry leader's characteristics that were listed, what does each of you perceive to be the most important ones that Freightco needs to establish?" After a lengthy discussion, the executives agreed that they perceived the most important characteristics to include providing services that have high value to customers; hiring and keeping highly capable employees; continuously improving services to meet needs and demands; and delivering what is promised.

Myron told the executives that while they had narrowed their original list, the characteristics stated must still be considered perceptions. He then instructed the executives that the perceptions had to be checked out through some objective means, such as conducting a benchmarking study, doing comparative analysis, accomplishing industry and market surveys, or other such processes. Clarence and the other executives agreed that the perceived characteristics needed to be evaluated and confirmed, and they agreed to meet with Myron on a separate project to accomplish that requirement.

Myron progressed to the second thinking strategy within the clarification stage—imagination. He asked the executives to provide their definition for imagination and received various responses including, "It's playing make-believe," "It's being creative," and "Imagination is being able to take something and change it around." Myron then pointed out that while imagination could include each of those things, he would encourage them to consider this definition: "Imagination involves the creation of new ideas for making Freightco the leader in their industry." He also emphasized that the executive team could only accomplish this by eliminating any attitudes of expertise. This comment promoted a significant amount of questioning and skepticism on the part of several executives because they believed they could not improve their current industry ranking if they didn't apply their expertise in the pursuit of the desired outcome. Myron responded by saying that while their concerns were somewhat valid, the point of minimizing and even eliminating the attitude of expertise helps achieve a greater application of the imagination thinking strategy. When expertise is applied during the clarification stage, there is a tendency for imagination to be stifled. For example, if the executives accomplished comparative analysis of services throughout the industry and the results are evaluated with a mind set of being an expert in the industry, then it is likely that some of the best ideas could be overlooked. Myron further emphasized this point by offering suggestions for how the executive team could promote and maintain imagination, and the thinking strategies that could be used to achieve imagination.

Myron moved the executives to the next part of imagination, and coached them in identifying and developing their imagination thinking strategies through visualization. Using Albert Einstein and Nikola Tesla as examples, Myron presented the importance of visualization as a thinking strategy for achieving greater imagination. He coached them through an exercise that helped them identify and construct their own thinking strategies for visualization.

The results of the visualization exercise were well received by the executives and they were fascinated by the amount of awareness and learning they had developed for their visualizing capabilities. Most of the executives were able to easily form and change their visualizations; however, a few of the executives did encounter some difficulty in forming visions in their mind. Myron took some time to further coach the executives by applying various techniques that helped in the creation and adaptation of visualizations. The results were gradual improvements in all of the executives' visual capabilities. However, they all agreed that they needed to further develop their ability to visualize. Myron emphasized the importance of practicing the visualization techniques over the next several weeks.

Having been exposed to the visualization thinking strategy, the executives were now ready to develop future visual imagery. Myron coached them through several exercises designed to practice this, specifically using the team's desired outcome of becoming the leader in their industry. For example, he had them establish a completion date for their outcome, and then had each executive create his or her own future vision to include a description of specific details about how the vision was successfully achieved. Each executive individually recorded the details of his or her vision. Then, Myron had them compare the details of each vision so the entire team could develop one common vision for the desired outcome to be achieved. This exercise took the remaining portion of the day to complete. Therefore, the executives decided to meet again within the week to begin the portion of the clarification stage dealing with thinking strategies that promote imagination through personal resource states.

Myron began the next meeting by highlighting the results achieved at the last session, particularly the visioning exercise. He then introduced personal resource states, and described how these techniques can create thinking that allows each person to develop, expand, and continuously improve imagination. Myron introduced the executives to techniques that achieve personal resource states through association and dissociation, recognizing and modifying characteristics of an internal state, and creating a mental stimulus or "signal."

The idea of imagination through the use of thinking strategies to create personal resource states was completely new and entirely different from what the executive team had ever experienced. Initially, there was skepticism and concern about the benefits of the techniques to their efforts. There was also hesitation on the part of some executives for accomplishing the personal resource state exercises. Myron recognized that fear of the unknown could produce the kinds of reaction exhibited by some of the executives. Myron patiently explained the application of the personal resource states using several examples and analogies, and responded to each executive's concerns before proceeding with the exercises. Clarence also emphasized that they had all agreed to fully develop their thinking strategies in new and better ways so they could increase their intellectual capital. Therefore, he suggested that they needed to identify and apply the thinking strategies that will move them beyond the status quo. Myron thanked Clarence and the other executives and moved on to coaching them through the exercises. As a result of the exercises, each executive developed a greater understanding for how he or she processed particular experiences and how that processing contributed to his or her personal resource states. They also developed an awareness for the distinctions that existed in their thinking, and then how to apply those distinctions for greater results. For example, Clarence shared the fact that he had learned how moving from a dissociated state to an associated state gave him a more positive feeling about a particular experience. He told the team how visualizations of future outcomes in which he saw things through his mind's eye were more satisfying, and he realized that when he had difficulty visualizing a future event in the associated state, it was probably due to some unanswered questions he had about getting to that future outcome.

Myron moved the executives to the intuition thinking strategy of the clarification stage, and introduced it as one of the most fascinating characteristics of great thinkers, yet one that has received little, if any, development within corporate environments. He then described the meaning of intuition and provided several examples of how intuition can and has been used by individuals in organizations. He also emphasized that because internal intuitive signals are unique, a specific process had not been established for teaching intuition. Therefore, Myron helped the executives develop an awareness about their own intuition capabilities, and coached them through several exercises for identifying their own intuitive signals and thinking strategies. Based on this new awareness and understanding, the executives were able to establish ways in which they planned to practice their intuitive abilities.

At this point in the session, Myron introduced the executives to the use of questioning strategies within the clarification stage. He stressed that the primary reason for using questioning strategies was to promote and maintain objectivity and help clarify meaning behind our perceptions. Questioning also reduces our attitude of expertise by causing us to be more curious and develop a better understanding about things and situations. Myron emphasized that the use of questioning would be important to the executives when clarifying various aspects of their desired outcome because it would formulate an understanding of root causes, establish the meaning and purpose of particular ideas, and promote an understanding of recommended solutions. Myron stressed the point that accurate information is the goal, and getting to the actual meaning of that information is essential.

Myron taught the executive team to apply questioning strategies in their work within the clarification stage. The executives learned and practiced questions that would promote the retrieval of accurate and specific information, and also applied the questioning formula of $(FUQ)^2$. Myron conducted several role play situations in which the executives used the questioning strategies to evaluate the meaning of their perceptions about the characteristics for becoming an industry leader. The result was further clarification for the meaning behind the characteristics that had been established.

After instructing the executives about the thinking strategies within the clarification stage, and helping them identify their own thinking strategies within the stage, Myron helped them apply their thinking to their desired outcome of becoming an industry leader. This was accomplished by (1) focusing on the perceptions of characteristics that were established, (2) reviewing the details of their shared visualization, (3) establishing the improvements they believed had to be implemented for achieving their desired outcome at the time they wanted it achieved, and (4) formulating and practicing the use of questioning strategies to create a greater understanding for the ideas to be generated.

The executive team was now ready to move to the generation stage. It was agreed that they would meet within four weeks. During that time, Myron and the executives planned to work together to establish an objective list of characteristics needed to become an industry leader, and clarify the details of their shared vision. Myron also met individually with the executives to coach them in the identification and application of thinking strategies within the clarification stage.

Applying the Generation Stage

Myron began the session with a review of the results achieved from previous sessions, and confirmed the characteristics that had been determined to be the most significant for achieving their industry leader's status. The executive team reported that results from a comparative analysis and industry survey confirmed the characteristics needing to be developed included (1) highly innovative services, (2) services that provide high quality and value to customers, (3) highly capable employees, (4) reliability and flexibility, and (5) continuous service improvements to meet ever-changing customer needs and requirements.

Having clarified information and data pertaining to their desired outcome, and having established a shared visualization of the outcome, as well as knowing that they had identified and practiced their clarification stage thinking strategies, the executives of Freightco were ready to move to the thinking strategies of the generation stage. Myron introduced the stage to the executives by explaining that it is the one that involves thinking strategies that develop creativity and the generation of ideas. During this session, the executives plan to identify and apply their thinking strategies for idea generation, and they will focus primarily on the creation of ideas for achieving their desired outcome of becoming an industry leader.

Myron began by helping the executives understand and appreciate the thinking strategies within the generation stage. Using examples from the life of Thomas Edison, Myron illustrated the thinking strategies that caused Edison to be one of the most gifted inventors. He then provided the executives with instructions about the thinking strategies of information processing, connections, and motivation. Myron explained that information processing thinking strategies enable people to acquire and manage data in ways that promote the generation of numerous ideas. He also explained that the thinking strategies of connections provide the ability to relate seemingly unrelated conditions or information, resulting in the generation of ideas. He then explained how motivation thinking strategies cause people to develop a strong desire to generate meaningful ideas and move toward action of the ideas. He pointed out that the generation stage also includes the techniques of paradigm expansion and relaxation for promoting the generation of ideas.

Myron introduced the information processing thinking strategies to the executives by emphasizing the fact that a tremendous flow of information exists in today's business environment. Therefore, specific thinking strategies must be clarified and applied to properly manage the information and deal with an ever-changing industry, because doing so increases performance, productivity, and the generation of ideas. Myron again used Edison as a model of someone who applied thinking strategies in the processing of information. He then reinforced the importance of each executive team member establishing his or her thinking strategies related to information processing. He explained that they will learn to identify and implement the techniques that reduce distraction and overload in order to achieve productive information processing. As a result, each executive will be able to use their thinking strategies to adjust to the demands that result in unwanted distractions and overload, thereby increasing the generation of ideas and performance.

Myron coached the executives through the internal and external techniques that relate to the thinking strategies of information processing. He emphasized that their use of individual strategies for processing information is neither positive nor negative, and the point was to identify the situations that cause distraction and overload so that more positive thinking can be applied to achieve the generation of ideas.

The executives agreed, through Myron's coaching, that connections would be a powerful and worthwhile thinking strategy for the generation of ideas. Myron explained how connections, as a thinking strategy, are often used yet rarely taught or promoted within the corporate environment. He also described the strong relationship that exists between connections and serendipity, and spent some time facilitating a discussion related to experiences of serendipity in each of their lives. The examples of serendipity that Myron provided gave the executives an appreciation for the application of connections within the generation stage. He then introduced the executives to the connections technique referred to as "linking," and coached them in several exercises that helped them develop and practice their ability to make connections between the learning and experiences they had previously acquired.

Before concluding the session, Myron presented an exercise in which the contents pages of several magazines were reviewed and connections were made between certain titles and the particular outcome that was being pursued. He brought a variety of magazines to the session and demonstrated the activity by having the executives practice making connections to their own situation. Following the demonstration, Myron instructed the executives to accomplish the same connections activity on their own by going to a library, randomly selecting at least five magazines, and selecting titles from the contents pages that stimulate ideas for their desired outcome of becoming the industry leader. Myron and the executives agreed to meet again within a couple of weeks.

Myron met the executives for another session, and he began by reviewing the connections they had made between the titles of magazine articles and their established outcomes. Myron facilitated the discussion of ideas and the executive staff discovered that they had generated a significant number of highly innovative ideas for developing the characteristics needed to achieve their role as the industry leader.

Next, Myron introduced the motivational thinking strategies of the generation stage. He explained Abraham Maslow's needs hierarchy model and described how the application of the five categories of needs—safety, security, social, esteem, and self-actualization—can assist the executives in determining the particular needs that must be individually satisfied to move them toward the generation of ideas and achievement of the desired outcome. Myron emphasized that motivation involves a positive mind-set and self-image, and is an important thinking strategy for creativity and the generation of ideas. Therefore, each executive's motivation is the result of an intense desire to achieve the outcome, and if that intense desire to achieve the outcome is not shared by each of the executives its likelihood for success is diminished. With this in mind, and using Maslow's hierarchy of needs model as the basis of several exercises, Myron coached the executive team to identify and clarify each of their motivational thinking strategies, particularly in relation to the desired outcome. As a result, the executive team was able to determine the characteristics of their motivational thinking strategies. Also, they shared their needs among the team and established a realistic understanding of and appreciation for how their individual needs related to achievement of the outcome. This exercise further solidified the executive team and increased their likelihood of success.

The techniques of reframing and paradigm expansion were introduced to the executive staff by Myron. He provided several examples of the techniques and then facilitated several exercises that helped the executives practice paradigm identification, expansion of boundaries, and expansion techniques. The executives found the paradigm expansion exercises to be extremely worthwhile as they enabled them to more fully consider their organization and entire industry in new and unique ways, which helped them generate a significant amount of ideas for developing industry leader characteristics.

Finally, Myron provided the executive team with relaxation techniques that promoted further generation of ideas. He also spent time coaching the executives on optimum environmental sourcing in order to help them determine the particular environments in which their most productive thinking and generation of ideas would occur. Myron and the executive team agreed to meet within a couple of weeks, at which time they would review the ideas generated for achieving their outcome, and begin the identification and application of thinking strategies within the prioritization stage.

Applying the Prioritization Stage

Myron reviewed results the executive team had achieved and discussed their identification and application of the thinking strategies. Clarence and several other executives shared examples of the successes and difficulties encountered as they had practiced identifying and applying their thinking strategies. Myron reassured them that practice is important and that their successes will breed additional successes.

When introducing the prioritization stage, Myron pointed out that while the generation of ideas can be a gratifying experience, it is important to establish the proper priority of the ideas for which action will be taken. He also emphasized that failure to prioritize can cause significant expenditures in both time and money. Therefore, it's important to identify and apply the thinking strategies that contribute to effective and efficient prioritization of ideas before moving onto the activation stage. Myron illustrated the importance of the prioritization stage through various examples of how top sales performers use impact analysis to arrange activities in the order of importance and according to the ultimate impact that each activity will have on the desired outcome. He then coached the executives to determine the risk and value of actions, or the impact, in relation to their outcome of becoming the industry leader.

Myron introduced the quick response and extended response methods for accomplishing impact analysis. He emphasized that both methods will be important to the executives as they progress toward their outcome. He explained how they would use the extended response method for prioritizing ideas related to the desired outcome, while the quick response method would be used at numerous times during the course of moving toward completion of the outcome.

With the help and coaching that Myron provided, the executive team applied impact analysis to the ideas they had previously established during the generation stage. As a result, their prioritization of ideas prepared them to move onto the activation stage. Myron and the executives planned to meet within the week.

Applying the Activation Stage

Myron and the executives began this session by reviewing the prioritization that was established for their ideas. He also took time to answer questions about the use of their thinking strategies and the application of the strategies for better thinking model. The executive team was now ready to develop the thinking strategies within the activation stage.

To illustrate the importance of the activation stage, Myron explained that the number of patents issued each year only represents the ones for which action had been taken. He told the executive staff to consider how many ideas have been generated without any action. Myron then described the five categories of thinking that tend to stifle action toward a desired outcome. Following discussions related to those categories, Myron used entrepreneurial profiles to provide significant detail about the five categories of thinking strategies that tend to promote action. He facilitated a discussion with the executives about the experiences they have had with their own activation thinking strategies.

Beginning with the category of vision, Myron coached the executives through several exercises that helped identify their capabilities for this thinking strategy. He emphasized the importance that visualization plays in creating future scenarios of a desired outcome, and illustrated the use of several visualization thinking strategies through examples and demonstrations. Myron helped them practice physical positioning, methods for stimulating their experiences, techniques for segmenting their visions, techniques for controlling interference during visualization, and methods for connecting their more dominant senses to the sense of sight. These exercises enabled the executives to develop and refine their visualization capabilities for use within the activation stage and in pursuit of their established outcome. Also, each executive developed his or her vision for the desired outcome of becoming the industry leader, and Myron coached the entire executive team to combine their individual visions into the formation of one group vision of the outcome.

Myron then introduced congruence as another one of the five categories of thinking strategies for taking action. He described to the executives how the thinking strategy of congruence can play a significant role in taking or not taking action in a particular situation, and how incongruence provides mixed messages and makes the achievement of a desired outcome extremely difficult. Then, Myron worked with the executives to clarify the thinking strategies each uses in relation to the congruencies and incongruencies they apply while moving toward achievement of a desired outcome. Once clarified, Myron coached the executives in methods that can be used to recognize and modify those particular thinking strategies when required.

The self-reliance category was introduced next by Myron, and he characterized this category as including thinking strategies associated with self-confidence, initiative, and decisiveness. He facilitated an exercise in which the executives determined their unique characteristics within each of these thinking strategies. As a result of the exercise, the executives developed a clearer understanding and appreciation for the strategies each uses to promote self-confidence, take initiative when appropriate, make decisions, or forego a decision in certain situations.

The executive team spent the next portion of their session with Myron discovering the thinking strategies that relate to risk-taking. Myron helped them identify and apply their risk-taking thinking strategies through demonstration and practice of the four ingredients which include anticipating obstacles, establishing contingencies, remaining flexible, and building confidence. Myron then coached the executives through several techniques that further developed their thinking strategies within each ingredient.

Having completed the sessions for the four stages of the strategies for better thinking model, the executive team decided to meet with Myron again to fully review the information and learning they had acquired about the awareness and application of their thinking strategies within each stage. They determined the need for additional group and individual coaching that would help develop their use of thinking strategies, and enable them to begin teaching the strategies for better thinking model to the organization's employees. They also decided that it was necessary to meet again to formulate the ideas and priorities that were established in relation to their outcome of becoming the industry leader. While the executives had developed a significant amount of innovative ideas pertaining to their outcome during the previous sessions, they wanted Myron to provide additional coaching that would apply thinking strategies to their outcome and move them to the actions necessary to achieve the industry leadership position.

MANUFACTURING BUSINESS APPLICATION

This scenario involves the creation of a training program for a medical products manufacturing division of an international pharmaceutical company (we will call the division Medico). The information provided in this scenario focuses primarily on the consultant's use of generation stage thinking strategies to develop useful ideas for the program's content and structure. The details of the scenario are based on discussions between the consultant (Betty), the director of organization development within the client organization (Arthur), and several members of the client's project team. Betty has previously accomplished projects within other divisions of the client organization. However, this is the first time she is working with Arthur and the members of the project team. Betty has significant background in performance consulting and strategies for better thinking, but Arthur and the other project team members have not been exposed to the stages of the strategies for better thinking model.

Medico was formed in the mid 1970s for the purpose of satisfying the growing needs of specialized medical products within hospitals. It has been extremely successful and profitable over the years, due primarily to its innovative research and development, quality manufacturing, and service-oriented approach to doing business. Medico is headquartered in a major eastern city of the United States, and its management is highly progressive and results oriented. While Medico has always been able to recruit, hire, train, and retain quality personnel, they had recently determined that the ability to make new employees productive within a short period of time has become a challenge due to the numerous changes in the healthcare industry and the rapid improvements in technology that continuously occur within their business. As a result of clarification of the issues related to this situation, the division's management has agreed to develop and implement a mentoring program that will assist new employees in quickly learning the division's business, products, systems, and processes, and thereby increase performance and productivity by at least 30 percent over current levels.

Applying the Clarification Stage

Betty's initial meeting with Arthur and the project team is conducted for the purpose of understanding the results of assessments and decisions that have led the division's management to approve the mentoring project. Betty also uses the discussion within this meeting to determine what their desired outcomes are for the project, how they intend to accomplish the project, and what expectations they have for her and themselves in making the project successful. Betty also uses the discussion as a way of developing an initial awareness of some of the thinking strategies that are used by the project team members.

For Betty, the initial meeting accomplishes many of the elements of the clarification stage. Her initial work with Arthur and the project team provides a collaborative beginning that is extremely valuable because it achieves the commitment and promotion required for the project's success. Betty uses this shared clarification to confirm the results of previous focus group sessions, interviews, and discussions. She also requests copies of documents and other materials that had been pertinent to establishing the project's requirements and useful in the development of the mentoring program. These activities and materials, combined with Betty's own internal thinking strategies, provide clarification of the perceptions, imagination, and intuition that will ultimately contribute to the program's creation.

Applying the Generation Stage

While working with the Medico's project team, Betty's experience in the generation stage thinking strategies resulted in a highly productive group process. Her use of the thinking strategies and other resources helped guide the team through many viewpoints, options, and alternatives for the structure and content of the mentoring program. The generation of ideas that resulted from this stage provided numerous choices and a variety of ways to approach the situations, resolve problems, manage the project, communicate with others, and ultimately create the program.

Betty and the team began to formulate an approach and create models for the mentoring program. In doing so, she applied several activities and exercises to help the team develop an awareness and application for the generation stage thinking strategies. As they discussed the models and training strategies that had been found in current literature, and as a result of their research with other organizations, they determined that most efforts lacked a spark, seemed too formal, had applications only to education or students, or fit just one specific type of business culture. Therefore, Betty facilitated a discussion among the team to bring out their thoughts, feelings, experiences, and ideas about mentoring. Betty asked the team to describe what they saw as the critical steps or stages in the mentoring process. Arthur described the mentoring process by what would take place and by the actions that would occur during each of the mentoring stages. Another team member suggested that there needed to be outcomes associated with each stage of the process.

Betty continued to facilitate additional thoughts from the team in an effort to create a graphic model for the mentoring process, including the likely stages and the words that would represent each stage. The team decided that searching for analogies might provide good direction in the creation of the mentoring stages. They began by using the analogy of buildings within a city, but soon found that the activities of each stage did not fit into the building terminology. One of the team members suggested a "medical-terms" model (since this was a medical products company), but they had difficulty finding terms that accurately fit the desired stages.

As the discussion and brainstorming continued with minimal results, Betty broke the pattern they were in to establish some points of view. Betty asked, "How many distinct stages were to be included in the process?" The answer was four. She then asked the team, "What types of processes or life situations have four stages?" "How about child development?" The responses included infancy (crawling), toddler (standing), child (walking), adolescent (leaving). The team decided that particular analogy didn't fit. Arthur asked, "What about the team building stages of forming, storming, norming, and performing that we've learned from past training sessions?" The team members considered that idea for a while but couldn't make it work for their mentoring process. Betty kept the team going by offering other thoughts, ideas, comparisons, and descriptive words that might encourage additional ideas and analogies. Numerous suggestions developed, but the team agreed that none had the impact they had hoped to establish.

Betty and the team members took a break and went to lunch. This time gave them an opportunity to relax, socialize, and get to know one another better. They returned to the conference room with renewed energy and confidence in their ability to come up with a workable model. After brainstorming several more ideas, they scored a hit with a travel analogy. All of the parts and pieces fell into place as if they were made for the company's mentoring model, and the descriptions of activities, outcomes, and processes were all in sync.

Betty congratulated the team and emphasized that whether they realized it or not, they had applied a variety of individual thinking strategies in the generation of ideas through collaboration resulting in a synergy that produced numerous ideas and options. Betty's use of the generation stage with the project team provided an environment in which everyone was a contributor and all ideas provided a springboard toward acquiring the best and most workable model for their mentoring process.

The creation of the mentoring model and its related analogy and terminology was the foundation for the subsequent design and development of the training program. Applying the generation stage thinking strategies saved hours and days of time in later stages that might have been spent searching for terms or visuals that could fit with a less than desirable process model. It also promoted excitement, camaraderie, and a volume of ideas among the team and further clarified their outcomes for the mentoring process.

Betty and the project team decided that they had accomplished a very successful session and decided to schedule another meeting to accomplish further development of the program.

Applying the Prioritization Stage

As Betty and the project team progressed through the generation stage, they had already begun to accomplish some elements of the prioritization stage. In fact, the results of their generation of ideas and program options led them to the selection of the analogy that they believed would provide the most appropriate results. It was an evolutionary process that yielded both numerous analogies and models, and also helped decision making regarding the best model to select.

In the case of Medico's training project, the prioritization stage involved the results of Betty's application of the clarification and generation stages. The prioritization stage in this situation actually progressed directly from the generation stage. Betty and the team began to judge, evaluate, sort, categorize, eliminate, and reduce the overwhelming amount of ideas and information into prioritized and manageable choices. Together, they determined what to choose, what to leave behind, what met their requirements, and how everything fit into their established outcome.

Applying the Activation Stage

In the case of Medico, the activation stage contained not only the act of selecting the desired analogy for the mentoring model, it also included the motivation that promoted action by the team to plan and accomplish the program's development. Each team member shared an intense desire to achieve the outcome of developing and implementing Medico's mentoring program. With this in mind, Betty suggested that in addition to the services she would provide toward the development of the mentoring program, it might be useful for the team to learn the thinking strategies associated with the activation stage of the strategies for better thinking model. Arthur and the project team agreed with the suggestion and they scheduled time to meet and accomplish that objective.

Several days later, Betty met with the project team to discuss the activation of the program after development was planned to be completed. She emphasized to the team members that they would need to act as internal consultants and view other members of the organization as their clients. Therefore, exactly how and when they planned to complete the project and work with others within the organization would be important in how they and their results would be judged. Betty emphasized that most clients, whether external or internal, have a desire for flexibility when working toward the achievement of project outcomes. Also, it is important to involve them in the project in ways that create buy-in, commitment, and the backing necessary to get the project moving steadily toward completion of the desired outcome. Getting internal clients and other decision makers involved throughout the entire activation stage will contribute to great reviews and excellent results.

The application of the activation stage to the project team's brainstorming and program development became the basis for the implementation of their pilot program. The outcomes, research, planning, creativity, assessment, and evaluation of the program's core elements came together during the actual creation of concepts, exercises, training methods, and writing of program materials. The pilot program was the application of the program, written in its "ideal" state and translating it into the "real" state. Betty and the project team determined they would evaluate their activation of the pilot program by considering questions such as, "Will the mentoring process and program materials as written work in a formal training situation?" "Will participants acquire the knowledge or skills required to meet the course objectives?" "Do the exercises achieve the learning objectives?" "Do the stages of the model visually convey the messages intended?" "What methods will ensure the retention of the learning?" These and other questions provided a framework from which the project team planned to evaluate the activation of their desired outcome.

Betty, Arthur, and the project team members progressed well through the development and implementation of the company's mentoring process. The program design, materials, and subsequent facilitation resulted in a process that achieved and exceeded Medico's desired outcome for increased performance and productivity of new employees.

Epilogue

Through continuous practice and experience with the stages of the strategies for better thinking model, our efforts to enhance and improve thinking strategies for ourselves and our clients provide significant results. The opportunities for identifying and applying thinking strategies in performance consulting projects and business growth or change situations are virtually limitless. Each context and application provides an opportunity to develop our thinking, adapt the use of the stages in different ways, vary the levels of time and energy in the stages depending upon the context, evaluate the risks and payoffs of situations, and apply newly identified thinking strategies to various contexts. We develop a sense of flexibility in order to practice and apply a myriad of thinking strategies for various circumstances.

Strategies for Better Thinking provides a unique and extremely helpful model that enables us to identify our thinking strategies, understand how and why we use particular strategies in certain contexts, and which thinking strategies result in the greatest levels of performance for us and our clients. Developing and applying thinking strategies within the clarification, generation, prioritization, and activation stages is a lifelong process that requires patience, constant practice, flexibility, and continuous improvement.

Bibliography

Adair, Gene. *Thomas Alva Edison: Inventing the Electric Age.* New York: Oxford University Press, 1996.

Baldwin, Neil. *Edison: Inventing the Century.* New York: Hyperion, 1995.

Barrett, Susan L. *It's All in Your Head.* 2d ed. Minneapolis: Free Spirit Publishing, 1992.

Beaumont, J. Graham. *Brain Power: Unlock the Power of Your Mind.* New York: Harper & Row, 1989.

Brian, Denis. *Einstein: A Life.* New York: John Wiley & Sons, 1996.

Bucky, Peter A. *The Private Albert Einstein.* Kansas City, Mo.: Andrews and McMeel, 1992.

Dilts, Robert B. *Strategies of Genius.* 3 vols. Capitola, Calif.: Meta Publications, 1994, 1995.

Ehrenberg, Miriam, and Otto Ehrenberg. *Optimum Brain Power: A Total Program for Increasing Your Intelligence.* New York: Dodd, Mead & Company, 1985.

Fischler, Martin A., and Oscar Firschein. *Intelligence: The Eye, The Brain, and The Computer.* Reading, Mass.: Addison-Wesley, 1987.

Foster, Jack. Illustrations by Larry Corby. *How to Get Ideas.* San Francisco: Barrett-Koehler, 1996.

Gardner, Howard. *Frames of Mind: The Theory of Multiple Intelligences.* 2d ed. New York: Basic Books, 1985.

Gunther, Max. *The Luck Factor.* New York: Macmillan, 1977.

Harman, Willis, and Howard Rheingold. *Higher Creativity: Liberating the Unconscious for Breakthrough Insights.* New York: Tarchar/Putnam, 1984.

Howard, Pierce J. *The Owner's Manual for the Brain: Everyday Applications from Mind–Brain Research.* Austin, Tex.: Leornian Press, 1994.

Husch, Tony, and Linda Foust. *That's a Great Idea: The New Product Handbook.* 2d ed. Berkeley, Calif.: Ten Speed Press, 1987.

Josephson, Matthew. *Edison.* New York: McGraw-Hill, 1959.

Kuhn, Thomas S. *The Structure of Scientific Revolutions.* 2d ed. Chicago: University of Chicago Press, 1970.

Leviton, Richard. *Brain Builders! A Lifelong Guide to Sharper Thinking, Better Memory, and an Age-Proof Mind.* West Nyack, N.J.: Parker Publishing, 1995.

Litvak, Stuart B. *Use Your Head: How to Develop the Other 80% of Your Brain.* Englewood Cliffs, N.J.: Prentice Hall, 1982.

Maslow, Abraham H. *Toward a Psychology of Being.* 2d ed. New York: Van Nostrand Reinhold, 1968.

————. *The Farther Reaches of Human Nature.* 4th ed. New York: Arcana, 1993.

Mattimore, Bryan W. *99% Inspiration: Tips, Tales & Techniques for Liberating Your Business Creativity.* New York: AMACOM, 1994.

Raine, D. J. *Albert Einstein and Relativity.* London: Priory Press, 1975.

Restak, Richard M. *The Brain.* New York: Bantam Books, 1984.

Russell, Peter. *The Brain Book.* New York: E. P. Dutton, 1979.

Sternberg, Robert J. *The Triarchic Mind: A New Theory of Human Intelligence.* New York: Viking Penguin, 1988.

————. *Successful Intelligence: How Practical and Creative Intelligence Determine Success in Life.* New York: Simon & Schuster, 1996.

Tesla, Nikola. *My Inventions.* 2d ed. New York: Barnes & Noble, 1995.

Tesla, Nikola and David H. Childress. *The Fantastic Inventions of Nikola Tesla.* Kempton, Ill.: Adventures Unlimited Press, 1993.

Thompson, Charles "Chic." *What a Great Idea! Key Steps Creative People Take.* New York: Harper Perennial, 1992.

Wachhorst, Wyn. *Thomas Alva Edison: An American Myth.* 2d ed. Cambridge: MIT Press, 1982.

Yepsen, Roger B., Jr. *How to Boost Your Brain Power: Achieving Peak Intelligence, Memory and Creativity.* 2d ed. Avenel, N.J.: Wings Books, 1992.

Index

ABOUT THE AUTHORS

Gerry H. Waller is President of PRO, a performance consulting firm located in Park Ridge, Illinois, and Managing Director of Promentum, a franchiser of performance consulting franchises. He is a Certified Master Practitioner of Neuro-Linguistic Programming and a Certified Management Consultant who helps individuals and teams increase performance and productivity.

Kathy A. Nielsen is President of Nielsen Associates, Inc., Buffalo Grove, Illinois. Her clients range from healthcare and financial services to government and electronics/telecommunications. She is the author of many training programs and several publications.